SIMPLE
ZEN

A Guide to Living Moment by Moment

SIMPLE
ZEN

A Guide to Living Moment by Moment

C. Alexander Simpkins Ph.D. • Annellen Simpkins Ph.D.

TUTTLE PUBLISHING
Boston • Rutland, Vermont • Tokyo

First published in 1999 by Tuttle Publishing, an imprint of Periplus Editions (HK) Ltd., with editorial offices at 153 Milk Street, Boston, Massachusetts 02109.

LIBRARY OF CONGRESS CATALOGING-IN-PUBLICATION DATA WILL BE FOUND AT THE END OF THIS BOOK.

Distributed by

USA
Tuttle Publishing
Distribution Center
Airport Industrial Park
364 Innovation Drive
North Clarendon, VT 05759
Tel: (802) 773-8930
Tel: (800) 526-2778

Japan
Tuttle Shuppan
RK Building, 2nd floor
2-13-10 Shimo-Meguro, Meguro-Ku
Tokyo, Japan 153-0064
Tel: (03) 5437-0171
Fax: (03) 5437-0755

Southeast Asia
Berkeley Books Pte. Ltd.
5 Little Road #08-01
Singapore 536983
Tel: (65) 280-3320
Fax: (65) 280-6290

Canada
Raincoast Books
8680 Cambie Street
Vancouver, Canada V6P 6M9
Tel: (604) 323-7100
Fax: (604) 323-2600

06 05 04 03 02 01 00   10 9 8 7 6 5 4 3 2
Book Design by Alicia Cech
Printed in the United States

We dedicate this book to our parents, Carmen and
Nathaniel Simpkins and Naomi and Herbert Minkin,
and to our children, Alura L. Simpkins and C. Alexander Simpkins Jr., and to all the
dedicated Zen masters whose lives and actions help communicate Zen to us today.

Carmen Z. Simpkins' abstract expressionist paintings
suggest mood, movement, and mysticism. Simpkins has
been painting for 75 years. Her first solo show took place in Camden, Maine, in
1962 at the Broadlawn Gallery.
She has exhibited throughout the world, and her works are in private collections in
Europe and America. She
continues to paint at her studio-gallery in
Sebastian, Florida.

CONTENTS

Zen Buddhism is a dynamic way to enhance living. Modern life demands our full attention, and there is often little time for anything else. The beauty of Zen is that it can help develop inner calm and better functioning even in the midst of a busy life. You do not have to make time for Zen—your Zen is with you all the time, enriching everything you do.

Zen points you back to your inner life, illuminating your true nature. As you become more adept at Zen meditation, it becomes integrated into your life, both at work and at play. "Not two!" the Zen masters would shout.

When we discovered Zen we were both graduate students, studying psychology and practicing martial arts. We delved deeply into the works of Suzuki, Dogen, Benoit, Watts, and other writers on Zen. We spent several years training our awareness in classes in New York City with Betty Keene and Charlotte Selver who conducted classes at the San Francisco Zen Center, and at the Tassahara Monastery. We spent long hours fully focusing our attention on the simplest of activities—breathing, sitting, standing whatever, to return our minds and bodies to natural functioning. We eagerly attended all the Zen lectures we could find, including those of Alan Watts. We continued to meditate as we searched for deeper understanding, discovering Zen through its many traditions, rather than narrowing to only one.

Zen gave us a perspective that opened new possibilities for psychology. In our studies in hypnosis with Milton Erickson, we saw a way of using Zen, that the unconscious was natural and intuitively intelligent. In fact it can be very wise. Our martial art, Tae Chun Do a form of moving meditation, continued to be a source of vitality and inner focus. We also took a Zen approach to the arts, specializing in wood crafting.

Just as we have been able to draw on Zen to enhance the quality of our lives, we hope that you, the reader, will find ways to make the most of Zen for yourself. There are many pathways into Zen, the capacity is already wired in. As the Zen masters say, "Nothing is missing."

About Simple Zen

This book is designed to help you understand Zen. It is divided into three interrelated parts. Part I gives the background and development of Zen, illustrated with classic enigmatic stories of great Zen masters to set you on the Path. Time lines are included in the end of the book for quick reference. Part II explains key themes, pointing you in the right direction. Part III shows you how to bring the insights of Zen into your life, through the practice of meditation and Zen arts, just as Zen practitioners have done for centuries.

You may choose to apply relevant Zen concepts to help you improve your life, or you may decide to follow its path more deeply and comprehensively. Start with where you are. However you decide to integrate the Zen Way into your life, let it open your potentials and guide you to simply living fully, moment by moment.

HOW TO USE THIS BOOK

Meditate regularly. This is the basis for discovering Zen. Meditation helps you clear away extraneous chatter, to focus on what really matters. When your mind is clear, you will find it easier to concentrate on what you are doing. You will be able to meet life's situations calmly and more energetically.

Zen is not just a set of concepts or a theory. It must be experienced. We encourage you to do the exercises. Read through the directions once or twice, then set the book aside and try them. When working with Zen arts, gather your materials first. Then set everything out and read through the directions before you begin. Concentrate on the quality of your mental attitude, not on the finished product or the goals. The journey is the essence of Zen: from an attuned, meditative awareness, you express yourself, your true self, at your best.

We invite you to enter the Path, and may you enjoy the journey!

PART I

Zen In Time

In the light of the moment we are Lost in eternal Now
As emptiness beckons mysteriously
—C. Alexander Simpkins

History is usually about dates and events of the past. Zen's history, however, is much more. Dialogues with pivotal masters, their pronouncements, and important incidents are windows that can show a doorway to Zen enlightenment. Stories about the founding Zen fathers were transformed into koans, teaching tools that transmitted the original spirit of Zen to later generations of students. When you read about how Bodhidharma stunned Emperor Wu, or when Lin-chi answered a student's question with a strike, or how Dogen heard enlightenment's wisdom from a cook, you get a vivid glimpse into the minds of these great teachers. Throughout Part I, as you learn about Zen's journey from its beginnings, you may begin your own journey on the Path to enlightenment.

Limestone/Budda, Chinese, sixth century

CHAPTER 1

Origins

Eyes closed, see your inner being in detail. Thus see your true nature.
— Vigyan Bhairava, ancient Hindu text

The origins of Zen reach back to ancient India and one of its indigenous religions, Hinduism. Early Hinduism guided people through a broad range of spiritual pathways. Many ancient writings described a myriad of Hindu practices and beliefs. The Vedas were written by the Aryan people who migrated from Persia and Russia to India around 2000 B.C. The Upanishads were brought to India between 800 and 600 BC. These ancient scriptures express Hinduism. Hinduism incorporated Yoga to put the philosophy into practice. Mind and body were enhanced through meditation. Yoga practices taught people to direct their attention away from the struggles of daily life, toward a higher plane of consciousness. The word yoga, from Sanskrit, means "to yoke or join" and signifies the goal of yogic practice: to link or join the individual spirit to the universal spirit. There are many forms of yoga. Each includes exercises to direct the mind toward higher development. Yoga was one of the earliest practices to use meditation as its primary method.

Buddhism grew from the broad and varied philosophies of the Hindu tradition. Siddhartha Gautama (563-483 B.C.), the founder of Buddhism, was the son of an Indian king. Prince Siddhartha was raised with every luxury at his father's palace. He read the Vedas and Upanishads and was taught Hinduism. Through his loving and careful upbringing, he developed into a highly sensitive and cultured young man. He married a beautiful princess who bore him a son. Siddhartha seemed to have everything anyone could want. He was happy. One day he took a trip outside his sheltered palace to survey the kingdom. He felt greatly disturbed by the poverty, sickness, and death he saw. He felt deep concern for the suffering in the world, and decided that he must leave his happy, luxurious palace life to seek answers for his people. Much to the chagrin of his wife and father, Siddhartha joined a group of ascetics, holy men who practiced self-denial in order to find wisdom. Siddhartha dressed in monks robes and fasted, as was the ascetic way. As he neared death he realized that if he died, he would never find the answers he sought. His search would have been in vain. He took food and water and vowed to continue his quest as he contemplated even more deeply. He would not stop until he had solved the problem of suffering. That night, he sat meditating under a bodhi tree. When dawn came, the first rays of the sun brought inner light to him. He realized that all the suffering in the world comes from our own minds and our own actions. The way to live is not to engage in extremes but to follow awarely along a middle path. With his enlightenment, Siddhartha Guatama became known as the Buddha, the Awakened One. He expressed his insight in these words:

> *I, Buddha, who wept with all my brothers' tears, whose heart was broken by a whole world's woe, laugh and am glad, for there is liberty! Ho! Ye who suffer! Know ye suffer from yourself. (Parulski 1976, 50)*

With time, Buddha formulated the path for all people to follow regardless of their social class. This was a radical departure from the structured caste system in place in India, which allowed only the religious caste, the Brahmins, to seek spiritual enlightenment.

Buddha's path was the Middle Way, neither engaging in extremes of self-indulgence nor of self-denial. He devised Four Noble Truths that could be readily followed by anyone who sincerely tried. First, people must realize that there is suffering in life. Second, they must recognize that the cause of this suffering is their own cravings. Third, suffering could be avoided by renouncing craving. And finally, the way to bring this about was to follow the Eightfold Path: right views, right aspirations, right speech, right behavior, right livelihood, right effort, right thoughts, and right contemplation. The practice of meditation, along with living a moral and ethical life, could bring about a peaceful existence devoid of suffering. Buddha's message drew many followers. According to legend, his entire family—his father, wife, and son—joined him in the search for enlightenment, helping to spread this new philosophy.

Zen evolved as a sect of Buddhism, as will become clear in later chapters. The spirit of Zen was born one day when Buddha was speaking to a group of disciples at Vulture Peak. All were listening to every word, searching for deeper meanings. As Buddha ended the sermon, he held up a flower and looked out over the audience. Only one disciple, Mahakasyapa, smiled. He experienced an awakening communicated directly from Buddha. This was the first direct transmission, mind to mind, the cornerstone of Zen. Words and studies are secondary to Zen enlightenment. Mahakasyapa became the Second Patriarch of Buddhism and was fundamental in carrying forth Buddha's teachings.

Buddhism continued to grow and develop in India. After Buddha's death, Mahakasyapa organized the First Council of Buddhist followers. They collectively recalled Buddha's teachings and memorized them so that his sermons would be remembered. These teachings, or sutras, became the basis of Buddhism.

Over time, the sutras were written, along with numerous interpretations. Followers began to divide into ideologically different sects, each with its own interpretation of Buddha's original enlightenment experience and how it should be expressed in practice. Inevitably, strong differences led to the splitting of Buddhism into two major divisions that still exist today: the Mahayana and the Hinayana (Theravada).

Mahayana Buddhism offered a viable path for the masses to follow. Unlike Hinayana Buddhism, which attempted to retain the purity of spirit in Buddha's original message by withdrawing from worldly life, Mahayana Buddhists stayed involved in everyday transactions. The ideal person in Mahayana, the bodhisattva, though seeking enlightenment, must turn away from paradise to become involved in helping others overcome suffering. Not until the entire world is enlightened can a bodhisattva withdraw from the world.

The new dimensions of meditative awareness through the practice of Buddhism spread to neighboring countries—China, Korea, and Japan. But in India, Hinduism reabsorbed Buddhism, so that Buddhism largely disappeared in its land of origin. By contrast, as Mahayana Buddhism spread to China, many innovations were incorporated that would develop even further in Japan. With time, Buddhism grew to become a worldwide religion, with many sects emphasizing different interpretations of what Buddha meant by his teachings. Zen Buddhism was one of the forms of Mahayana Buddhism that developed in China. Drawn directly from Buddha's enlightenment, Zen captures the spirit of the founder to transmit enlightenment to anyone who is willing to seek.

CHAPTER 2

Early Zen in China and Korea

When the hubless wheel turns, Master or no master can stop it.
It turns above heaven and below earth, South, north, east, and west.
— *Mumonkan,* Case 8, in Reps 1994, 124

For centuries, the threads of Taoism and Confucianism had been intimately woven into the fabric of Chinese cultures. Both are thought to have had their origins around the sixth century B.C., over six hundred years before Buddhism arrived in China and more than a thousand years before Zen began. Buddhism might not have been as widely accepted if the Chinese people had not already been practicing these earlier religions, which paved the way for Buddhist thought. The two philosophies complement each other perfectly. Taoism has been called the Way of Heaven. Confucianism has been called the Way of Man. Taoism guided people spiritually, helping them return to the source, the mysterious Tao that is in the deepest nature of everything and everyone. Confucianism offered a compass for ethical behavior, to sincerely follow the golden mean, chung, thereby discovering

Landscape painting depicting a hidden forest monastery

both inner and outer harmony. From China, Buddhism made its way to Korea, and then to Japan.

BUDDHISM COMES TO CHINA

Mahayana Buddhism took its first steps on Chinese soil during the first century A.D. Beginning in outlying areas of China, Buddhism gradually spread into the heart of the country via well-established trade routes. China avidly embraced Buddhism, and by A.D. 500, Buddhism was even more popular in China than it had been in India.

The Chinese added their own unique perspective, blending Buddhism with Confucianism and Taoism. Chinese translators who introduced Buddhism often couched it in Taoist terms to make it more understandable and easier to assimilate. For example, Chinese translators substituted the word Tao for the Sanskrit word *marga*, or "Path." The Chinese had long believed that Tao, a mysterious Oneness, was the foundation and essence of all being. This old Chinese concept merged with the new Buddhist ideas, giving Chinese Buddhism a flavor never quite intended by the Sanskrit texts.

Many new Buddhist sects emerged in China around the time that Zen began. In fact, the years between A.D. 500 and 800 were the most creative for Chinese Buddhism. T'ien-t'ai (Tendai), Pure Land, and Hua-yen were three sects that began in China and would live on in Japan and Korea as prominent forms of Buddhism. Zen was also founded during this period.

ZEN BEGINNINGS

Returning to the root,
we get the essence.
— *"Hsin Hsin Ming," Blyth 1969, 101*

Without the creative inspiration of the Chinese people combining with the religious mysticism of India, Zen as we know it would not have come to be. Zen blends the spirit of emptiness from Buddhism with the true nature of Tao, a mysterious Oneness that permeates and guides everything. Zen emerged as a new Mahayana Buddhist sect in A.D. 500, guiding people to enlightened experience through the practice of meditation. In fact, Zen is the Japanese word for meditation. The Chinese word is Ch'an, which is how Zen was known to the people of China. The regular practice of meditation continues to be the cornerstone of Ch'an and Zen, as it was in the beginning.

The First Patriarch of Zen was an Indian Buddhist monk who was given the name Bodhidharma by his teacher of Buddhism, Pranatara. It was Pranatara's dying wish that Bodhidharma travel to China and spread the teachings of Mahayana: The mind is the buddha. Bodhidharma followed his teacher's wish and made the long, difficult journey to China.

Once on Chinese soil, Bodhidharma traveled around the countryside preaching his method. He said:

I don't talk about precepts, devotion, or ascetic practices...These are fanatical, provisional teachings. Once you recognize your moving, miraculously aware nature, yours is the mind of all buddhas. (Pine 1989, 42-43)

Buddha is Sanskrit for "aware." Bodhidharma believed that all of your awareness—whether seeing, hearing, moving your arms and legs, even blinking—is intimately identified with buddha nature. "This nature is the mind. And the mind is the Buddha. And the Buddha is the path. And the path is Zen" (Pine 1989, 29).

Emperor Wu, of the Liang dynasty (502-57), heard about this radical monk from India and summoned him for an audience. Emperor Wu was a generous patron of Buddhism and zealously supported Buddhist doctrine. He said to Bodhidharma, "I have built many Buddhist temples and distributed many scriptures. Have I acquired merit?"

Bodhidharma answered, "Absolutely none." Bodhidharma believed that merit derives from wisdom, which is cultivated by meditation, not external acts.

Emperor Wu then asked, "Who then is before me?"

Bodhidharma replied, "I do not know!"

Bodhidharma's answers shocked and confused the emperor, who did not understand that Bodhidharma was attempting to demonstrate his commitment to the purity and simplicity of Zen. Buddha mind, the state of consciousness discovered through meditation, is the same for all people, peasants and kings alike. Everyone has a buddha mind, part of the Oneness, without any hierarchy or superiority. Anyone can become Buddha through meditation's transformation.

Bodhidharma quickly became disillusioned by the lack of understanding and commitment in those he encountered. According to legend, he traveled to a cave near the Shaolin temple in Hunan Province and sat facing a wall, meditating for nine years, speaking to no one. Word spread that there was an intensely devoted monk deep in meditation who had great wisdom. Many came, hoping to learn from him, but Bodhidharma sat quietly, gaze fixed. No successor was among them. No one was worthy.

Finally, one man, Hui-k'o (487-593), was said to have cut off his own arm and handed it to Bodhidharma as a symbol of his absolute dedication to the Way. With this gesture from Hui-k'o, Bodhidharma helped him realize enlightenment and accepted him as a worthy successor. Hui-k'o became the Second Patriarch of Zen, carrying forth the spirit of Zen.

Zen was taught personally. Enlightenment was communicated directly from teacher to student, much like it was first taught by Buddha to Mahakasyapa. This form of learning continues today: Zen wisdom is still communicated through contact between teacher and student and is called direct transmission.

The early Chinese patriarchs were well versed in the Chinese classics, and they integrated Zen with the accepted philosophies of China, particularly Taoism. Each man contributed in his own way. The Third Patriarch, Seng-ts'an, (d. 606) composed the first Zen poem, "Hsin Hsin Ming, Inscribed on the Believing Mind," which clearly shows the integration between Buddhism and Taoism to form the unique synthesis that is Zen. Taoism sees all phenomena in the world as yin and yang opposites. Buddhism views all as emptiness. Zen blends the two:

> *When activity is stopped and passivity obtains*
> *This passivity again is a state of activity.*
>
> *...The activity of the Great Way is vast.*
> *It is neither easy nor difficult. (Blyth 1969, 100-101)*

The Fourth Patriarch, Tao-hsin (580-651), organized the first Zen community; here, monks lived separated from their families and society. Hung-jen (601-674), the Fifth Patriarch, inspired many great Zen masters who founded sects of Zen that endured for several generations. His most famous pupil, Hui-neng, helped launch Zen toward its vital and enduring future.

THE SIXTH PATRIARCH

Bodhidharma is considered the founder of Zen, but Hui-neng (638-713), the Sixth Patriarch, brought about a new emphasis. Unlike all the previous patriarchs, who were highly educated, Hui-neng was said to be a poor, illiterate firewood cutter. One day, just after having sold some of his firewood in the marketplace, he came upon a man reciting one of the most famous Mahayana sutras, the Diamond Sutra (Jewel of Transcendental Wisdom). This Sutra, when carefully studied, can bring about a reorientation of thinking in the Buddhist way. Hui-neng listened to the words and felt a profound change take place. Unexpectedly, and in a flash of sudden insight, he was enlightened. The idea that anyone, even a simple peddler, could become suddenly enlightened became one of the seminal ideas in Hui-neng's Zen.

Hui-neng journeyed to the temple of Hung-jen, the Fifth Patriarch, to deepen his understanding. Monasteries usually excluded uneducated people, but Hui-neng was accepted as a lay monk and given the job of pounding rice and splitting firewood. Hung-jen recognized that his new student had natural talent.

Eventually, the Fifth Patriarch was ready to retire and appoint a successor. Hung-jen asked his students to compose a poem that epitomized their insight. Shen-hsiu, the senior student, was naturally expected to be given the official robe and bowl that signifies direct transmission. Shen-hsiu's poem read:

Our body is the bodhi tree
And our mind a mirror bright
Carefully we wipe them hour by hour
And let no dust alight. (Price & Mou-lam 1990, 70)

On hearing this poem, Hui-neng felt a deeper insight and composed his own poem:

There is no bodhi tree
Nor stand of a mirror bright
Since all is void,
Where can the dust alight? (Price & Mou-lam 1990, 72)

The Master listened to both poems and recognized Hui-neng's wisdom. According to the account of what happened, as written in the Platform Sutra, by Hui-neng's disciple, Hung-jen believed that his disciples would not accept an illiterate lay monk as his successor, so he secretly sent Hui-neng off to the south to start his own branch of Zen. Meanwhile, he also recognized Shen-hsiu who had come to merit the promotion through his years of devoted service and study. Shen-hsiu, traveled north and founded the Northern School. He taught that calm, quiet meditation gradually lead practitioners to an enlightened life. Following a bitter conflict with the Southern school led by Hui-neng's disciple Shen-hui (670-762). The direct line of Northern Zen did not last beyond two more generations of students. Echoes of the quiet Zen of Shen-hsiu resonate to this day in the practice of Soto Zen, where daily quiet meditation is primary.

By contrast, Hui-neng's Southern School was active, guiding students to sudden awakenings. Hui-neng accepted students of any class or background because he firmly believed, based on his own experience, that "the essence of mind is already pure and free" (Price and Mou-lam 1990, 73). Neither long study nor unusual talent was necessary to achieve enlightenment. Anyone, from a lowly peasant to a royal king, could have enlightenment, forever transforming life, once they realized this simple truth. Hui-neng's Southern School became the dominant force. Most modern schools of Zen trace their roots back to Hui-neng.

T'ANG DYNASTY (618-907): THE FLOWERING OF ZEN

Following Hui-neng, Zen spread throughout the country, with many great masters who expressed themselves freely. The T'ang period was one of the most creative and innovative for Zen in China. During this period, Zen masters found ways to teach without using rational explanations, often without words. Instead, the monks took action by swinging a stick or shouting.

Students in this period could expect the unexpected from their teachers. They were called upon to stretch the limits of understanding by answering bizarre questions and solving strange puzzles. In the spaces between, when confusion and surprise left a gap, the light of enlightenment could suddenly break through.

Ma-tsu (709-788) was one of the many great masters of this period. His work, along with that of other innovative teachers, shaped the development of Zen in China and later became a backdrop for Korean and Japanese Zen.

Ma-tsu was a dynamic and forceful individual who was the first Zen master known to use shouting to bring his students to enlightenment. One of his teachers was a student of Hui-neng, putting Ma-tsu in direct line with the sudden enlightenment tradition.

One famous exchange between Ma-tsu and his teacher illustrates a primary understanding in the Southern School of Zen. As a young student, Ma-tsu was meditating ardently in pursuit of a pure mind. The Master asked him, "Why are you sitting so long in meditation?"

Ma-tsu replied, "I am hoping to become a buddha."

With this, his teacher picked up a tile and began rubbing it with a stone. Ma-tsu looked at him, puzzled. "What are you doing, Master?"

The Master answered, "I am polishing this tile until it becomes a mirror."

This made no sense to Ma-tsu, so he asked, "How can you make a mirror from a tile?"

The teacher answered, "Exactly! How can you make a buddha by trying to purify your mind?"

This communicated the essence of Hui-neng's Zen: Your original nature is already pure, just as it is. Why try to cleanse it? Throughout his life, Ma-tsu continued to teach that the mind is the buddha.

One of Ma-tsu's students, Pai-chang (720-814), created rules for everyday life in the Zen monastery. All monks must take vows to live an absolutely ethical life. But vows were not enough. They must also do some form of work along with daily meditation. He believed that if your mind is the buddha, then you should be able to bring this understanding into all aspects of life, including work. After all, Hui-neng was a firewood cutter.

One day, Pai-chang's students, thinking they would give their Master a rest from working in the field, hid his gardening tools. Pai-chang refused to eat. Finally the monks had no choice but to return his tools. Pai-chang told them, "A day without work is a day without food."

This became the motto for all the Zen monasteries that followed. The work the monks did raising crops, building monasteries, and taking care of their own needs as an ethically strong community allowed Zen to evolve independently, through all kinds of political climates. Thanks to the monastic tradition of self-sufficiency that Pai-chang initiated, Zen was not harmed by the great obliteration of Buddhism that took place in China from 841 to 845.

Huang-po (d. 850), who is also known by his Japanese name, Obaku, was a student of Pai-chang. He helped his disciples experience the true nature of the Buddha mind: absolute emptiness. "Develop a mind which rests on nothing whatever," Huang-po explained (Blofeld 1994, 153). Huang-po urged his students: "Mind is filled with radiant clarity, so cast away the darkness of your old concepts. Rid yourselves of everything" (Blofeld 1994, 160). The Way is not something to be reached by sutra studies or pious rituals, he taught, and described enlightenment as "A perception, sudden as blinking, that subject and object are one, will lead to a deeply mysterious wordless understanding; and by this understanding will you awake to the truth of Zen" (Blofeld 1994, 161).

Lin-chi, Rinzai Zen

Huang-po was a teacher of Lin-chi (d. 866), who became one of the most influential Zen masters of all time and the founder of the Rinzai School of Zen. Lin-chi, called Rinzai in Japanese, could be considered a humanist. He believed that people are perfect just as they are. He called this "the man of no rank" because he felt that nothing is missing. Why pursue external titles, positions, and learnings? He advised his disciples, "Just be ordinary. Don't put on airs" (Watson 1993, 192). Ultimately, Zen enlightenment comes from within, naturally.

Lin-chi told his disciples, "Since you students lack faith in yourself, you run around seeking something outside" (Dumoulin 1990, 191). He believed that people should turn the light of awareness inward to find the true Way.

Seeking outside for something
This hardly becomes you!
If you wish to know your original mind,
don't try to join with it, don't try to depart from it! (Watson 1993, 62)

Lin-chi spoke to his disciples in everyday language, but, like many masters of the T'ang period, he also used sudden, dramatic actions—such as shouting, kicking, or even a blow with a stick—to help students shake off their inhibiting, rigid sense of reality.

A monk once asked Lin-chi, "Tell me what is the essence of Buddhism?" Lin-chi held up his fly wisk. The monk shouted. And then, suddenly, Lin-chi struck him. There was no room for intellectualizing. The student found enlightenment in that instantaneous experience.

Although Lin-chi taught in a small rural monastery, his lectures were later recorded by a lay disciple of the Rinzai school, Li Tsun-hsu (d. 1038), as a discourse, called the *Lin-chi Lu,* which later expanded into the *Rinzairoku* in Japanese. Lin-chi's school of Zen flourished, in part, because his wise teachings were transcribed and passed along. In realizing that the everyday, sincere, ordinary human being lacks nothing, Lin-chi helped generations of Zen practitioners discover that the Way of Zen meant being true to their nature.

THE SUNG DYNASTY IN CHINA (960-1279): ZEN SPREADS

Zen's most creative masters lived and taught during the T'ang dynasty, but more people practiced Zen than ever before during the Sung dynasty, when Zen became institutionalized as a nationally recognized and practiced religion. Zen monks taught at the imperial court for the first time, and the government funded a state system of temples, called the Five Mountains and Ten Temples. Two major schools became dominant: Lin-chi's Rinzai and Ts'ao-tung, later to be known as Soto in Japan.

In order to accommodate the large number of students who wanted to learn Zen, the masters devised new ways to teach. Even though they could no longer attend to each person individually, they still wanted to remain true to the spirit of Zen by bringing about direct transmission, mind to mind, the foundation for learning Zen. To solve this problem, the enigmatic stories and riddles that were used by the T'ang masters were written down into what became known as kung-ans (koans in Japanese), which translates as "public record." Students were given a Zen master's koan to think about in meditation to help them evolve. Koans were often paradoxically mysterious and puzzling. Only when conscious thinking was set aside could the koan be truly "penetrated," thereby stimulating enlightenment. With time, koans were collected into books, such as the *Mumonkan* (Gateless Gate) and the *Hekiganroku* (Blue Cliff Record).

Bodhidharma's encounter with Emperor Wu became the first koan in the *Hekiganroku*. These books were brought to Japan and helped to keep the spirit of the early Zen masters alive. Later, the renowned Japanese Zen monk Hakuin systematized koan practice, creating a method that is still used today in Rinzai Zen. Koans force the individual to discover a new way of thinking. We will work with koans later in this book.

Rinzai and Soto differed in how they taught Zen. Rinzai practitioners believed koans required active searching and intense involvement, to bring about enlightenment in a flash. Koans were a dynamic teaching aid to open and develop enlightenment,(satori in Japanese) for Rinzai students.

One of the most prominent Rinzai masters of the Sung period, Ta-hui (1089-1163), believed so strongly in the value of the inner struggle that he burned every copy of the *Hekiganroku,* written by a member of his teacher's school, because he thought it was too explicit. Fortunately, a copy was discovered two hundred years later and the book was reissued. Ta-hui developed a method of koan practice called hua-t'ou, in which the essence of the koan becomes the focus of meditation, with very powerful results.

Early Soto practitioners criticized this application of koan practice, claiming that koan study can point students' attention away from meditation, the true source of enlightenment. They drew from the original message of Bodhidharma and believed that sudden enlightenment was not the goal. It was better to practice daily meditation and foster a deep, continuous awareness, calm and clear.

LATER PERIOD

The Sung period was the apex of Zen's popularity in China. By the time of the Ming Dynasty (1368-1644) in China, Zen began to merge with other Buddhist sects.

Early Buddhism Leads to Korean Son (Zen)

Korea learned of Zen directly from China, before it went to Japan, and Zen played a prominent role in its history. Korea was introduced to Buddhism from China during the Three Kingdom period (37 B.C. - A.D. 668) of its history. The royal houses of all three kingdoms welcomed Buddhism in the hopes that it would help to bring greater peace and unity. Buddhism was woven into the fabric of Korean life as the Korean peninsula continued its close interactions with China.

Won Hyo (617-686) popularized Buddhism in Korea. This uninhibited and free-spirited monk wrote extensively on Buddhism, especially topics concerning faith, interacting with nobles and commoners alike. His writings are still being translated today. He is revered by Korean Zen masters as well as Korean Buddhists as a great teacher even though he was unconventional. After enlightenment, he did not withdraw into a monastery. Instead, he spent his time helping people in bars and places that lacked social approval. After all, those were the people who needed help, not the virtuous! He taught followers how to meditate deeply to be happy and enlightened, whatever their circumstance. He encouraged a syncretic trend in Korean Buddhism, inspiring the common person to harmony and self-acceptance. Enlightenment should be for everyone, he believed, not just the elite.

KOREAN SON DEVELOPS THROUGH DYNAMIC MASTERS

Koreans traveled to China and studied Zen under Ma-tsu's students during the T'ang dynasty period. Upon their return to Korea with their Zen enlightenment, these monks founded remote Zen monasteries in the sparsely populated mountain regions. These monasteries became known as the Nine Mountain Schools, the foundational structure for Zen in Korea. Toui (d. 825) was the founder of Porim-sa temple on Mount Kaji, the first of the Korean mountain schools of Zen.

KOREA'S GREATEST ZEN MASTER: CHINUL

Chinul (1158-1210) was recognized not only in Korea but also in China as one of Korea's greatest Zen monks. He taught that there is a sentient intelligence within each person, the principle behind seeing and hearing: the individual mind, the buddha-nature. This principle is what makes it possible for human beings to become enlightened. In Chinul's system, human beings are capable of using all aspects of their intelligence for enlightened living. Each has its place in the grand scheme of buddha nature.

Chinul carefully expounded the need for both gradual and sudden approaches to enlightenment. Sudden enlightenment, first explained by Hui-neng, happens in an instant of direct, intense realization. But learning does not stop with the first light of insight. Gradually, over time the student develops, deepening the enlightenment. Gradual cultivation relates to the relative rational, or sign-oriented, aspects of our everyday world. All external sign-oriented phenomena are invitations to experience a deeper, truer understanding at the absolute level of wisdom. The path of enlightenment is here and now, through symbols and words, as well as through experience.

Chinul's teachings were specific and detailed, offering techniques so that the needs of students with varied intellectual and spiritual capacity could be met. For example, he thought not-thinking meditation was helpful for those who had attained spiritual awakening, but he also believed the intellect was needed to help disentangle students from negative habits. This was part of the sudden awakening/gradual cultivation process he believed was essential for sustaining enlightenment. As he explained to his students: "Hence sudden awakening and gradual cultivation are like the two wheels of a cart: neither one can be missing" (Seung Sahn 1987, 99).

Chinul's approach to Zen technique emphasized and developed Ta-hui's analytic adaptation of koans, or hua-t'ou, calling this tool of meditation hwadu. Hwadu are shorter than koans because the koan story is removed, thus leaving only the topic. Students were instructed to focus attention on the hwadu as a kind of yogic concentration to block out distraction and interpretation and thus achieve a deep focus on the essence of the koan. The discursive intellect was bypassed. Chinul felt that this method was a direct path to enlightenment.

Chinul's school of Son was called the Chogye, which is the Korean term for the sect of Hui-neng. Chinul offered a unified group to which the separate, often contending, schools could belong, with a harmonizing rationale. He invited monks from the different schools to meet in the forests for group meditation.

Although unity did not come to Korean Buddhism for quite some time, it remained an important goal for later monks. T'aego Pou (1301–1382), along with the influence of King Kongmin's royal decree (1345), encouraged the Zen monks to unite as one order, as Chinul had done before him. Unity gradually came to be a political reality, but hundreds of years, as well as the decrees of more than one monarch, were needed to bring it to fruition.

LATER DEVELOPMENTS

In Korea, the tides turned against Buddhism, forcing those who continued the traditions to retreat to the remote mountain temples. Although the life cycle of Zen as an independent sect of Buddhism was ebbing in China and Korea, it would find new life in Japan, where it was just beginning to take root.

CHAPTER 3

Middle Period in Japan

*In the world of the truly pure, there is no separation. Why wait again
for another time? The tradition of Vulture Peak has arrived.
The authority of the Dharma needs no one.*
—Muso, national teacher of Japan, in Dumoulin 1990, 163

EARLY BUDDHISM IN JAPAN

Japan was prepared for Zen by the earlier introduction of Buddhism in
552. During the reign of Emperor Kinmei, Korea first introduced Buddhism
to Japan with its gift of a golden statue of Buddha. Several forms of Buddhism
were brought to Japan by a succession of emperors. Prince Shotoku Taishi
(572–621) incorporated Buddhism into the Japanese constitution. Prince
Shotoku was fond of the Vimalakirti Sutra, which portrayed a householder
who became a bodhisatva. This sutra explained that even a layperson could
find enlightenment, setting the stage for Zen. Everyday life can be an opportunity to live morally and stay focused meditatively. Prince Shotoku became

Fukurokuju by Hakuin

the most renowned interpreter of the Vimalakirti Sutra in Japan.

Buddhism soon grew to be a well-established institution that was supported by the government of Japan. Buddhist monks were given political influence and played an active role in court policies. Shingon and Tendai Buddhism had attracted royal support and patronage for hundreds of years and became the dominent forms of Buddhism.

As time passed, the doctrines and rituals of Buddhism evolved to become more and more complex. Tendai Buddhism emphasized meditation as part of a triad of practices along with performance of rituals and elaborate analysis. At first, Zen was linked to Tendai. Eventually, Zen evolved to become its own distinct discipline, the Rinzai tradition.

MYOAN EISAI BRINGS RINZAI ZEN

Zen was brought to Japan by several monks between the years A.D. 600 and 800, but it did not take hold until a dedicated Buddhist monk named Myoan Eisai (1141-1215) founded a Zen temple that endured.

Eisai had been guided toward a religious life from his early years. His father entrusted Eisai's education to the monks, and at age fourteen he entered the monkhood, shaved his head, and was ordained on Mount Hiei, near Kyoto. He eagerly learned Tendai, a form of Buddhism brought from China that taught the "Threefold Truth: Absolute truth of Emptiness, Relative truth of phenomenas, and the Middle Way between."

Eisai could see that Buddhism was in need of reform, and in April 1168 he made a pilgrimage to China to deepen his knowledge. He hoped to renew and revitalize Buddhism, which was failing in Japan. He took with him a Shingon monk named Chogen (1121-1200). Together they visited Mount T'ien-t'ai, the source of Tendai Buddhism, where they learned that the meditation that was part of Tendai practice originated in Zen temples in China. Upon his return to Japan, Eisai founded a new line of Tendai called Yojo. The regent Hojo Mikkyo declared Eisai the patriarch of this line.

Twenty years later, Eisai returned to China to retrace Buddhism to its roots in India. However, his plans were thwarted when he was refused a visa to enter India, so he did the next best thing and studied Zen in China. Zen claimed to have the true dharma, transmitted directly, over the centuries, from Buddha himself. Eisai believed that this flourishing Chinese sect could revitalize Japanese Buddhism. He returned to Mount T'ien-t'ai where he found a master of the Rinzai sect, Hsuan Huai-ch'ang (Koan Esho, in Japanese), the eighth generation of the Huang-lung (Oryo, in Japanese) line of Lin-chi (Rinzai). He followed this master when he left the temple to reside at Mount T'ien-t'ung. Through Zen meditation, Eisai found the deeper inspiration he had been seeking. He received a certificate, insignia of succession, as dharma heir of the Huang-lung line.

Eisai returned to Japan, ready to spread the message of the dharma through Zen. He landed at Hirato, a port on Kyushu, one of the islands of Japan, and began to propagate Zen. Eisai wrote a persuasive treatise about the value of Zen entitled *Kozen Gokokuron* (Treatise on the Spread of Zen for the Protection of the Nation) (1198). He believed that the large city of Kyoto would be the best place to establish Zen. But Eisai ran into resistance from the Tendai and Shingon establishment. Roben, a Tendai monk from Hakasaki, Kyusu, persuaded the emperor's court to issue an interdict against Eisai's new Zen sect. Eisai left the city and in 1195 founded Shofoku-ji, a monastery in Hikata that was under the protection of the Shogun Minamoto Yoritomo. Later, in 1202, he established a temple in Kyoto, the Kennin-ji Monastery, which became an important center for Zen.

Eisai's temples endured. He is given credit for bringing Zen to Japan, and also for introducing tea—he carried tea seeds back with him from China and planted the first tea garden on monastery grounds. This would eventually lead to the development of tea drinking as a Zen art.

Although Eisai's Zen was always mixed with Tendai, he had planted the seeds. His students carried on the Rinzai Zen traditions that Eisai had started, firmly rooting Zen in Japan.

DOGEN ESTABLISHES SOTO ZEN

One of Eisai's students, Myozen, studied Tendai Buddhism before he joined Eisai's temple. He trained with Eisai, and became his number one disciple. After Eisai died, Myozen determined that he would follow his master's footsteps and go on a pilgrimage to China to the temple where Eisai found enlightenment.

Dogen (1200–1253) was a young student of Myozen at Kennin-ji Monastery at this time. He encouraged Myozen to make the trip and asked to accompany him. Soon after landing in China, Dogen met a cook who opened his eyes to Zen. The cook was an elderly tenzo monk, which means he was the monk in charge of cooking. The cook had come to the ship to buy Japanese mushrooms for the monastery. Dogen, who was interested in talking to this Chinese monk, asked him to stay and talk about Buddhism.

The tenzo monk replied: "I'm sorry, but I must return to the monastery as soon as I purchase the mushrooms. Otherwise, the meals will not get done. Even though I am old, I hold the position of tenzo, and cooking is what I do. And also, I did not receive permission to stay."

Dogen tried to persuade him saying, "Wouldn't it be better to meditate and study koans? What good does it do to work so hard at cooking?"

The tenzo monk laughed, "Good foreigner, you seem to be ignorant of the true meaning of Zen!"

Naively, Dogen asked, "What is the true meaning of Zen?"

The monk answered, "Once you can answer your own question, you will understand Zen."

Dogen did not yet understand that Zen is in everything we do, be it cooking, cleaning, or sitting in meditation. He was so moved and inspired by the cook that he later considered cook an honored position at his monasteries.

Myozen and Dogen went to the temple where Eisai had his enlightenment. But Dogen did not feel satisfied, and so he ventured forth to seek a deeper understanding. He heard about Ju-ching (1163-1228), an abbot at the T'ien-t'ung temple who was considered to be a master of pure Zen. Ju-ching valued sitting awarely in meditation above all else. As a follower of the T'sao-tung tradition (Soto Zen), Ju-ching was against Rinzai's use of koans and its emphasis on sudden enlightenment. Dogen spent many long hours meditating, but was unable to become enlightened. One day while he was meditating another student fell asleep. The Master reprimanded the student saying, "How do you expect to be enlightened when you are dozing?" Upon hearing this, Dogen experienced enlightenment. Suddenly, he understood what the cook had meant: the quality of practice was most important. This became one of the primary axioms in the teachings of Dogen's Soto Zen: Practice is not separate from enlightenment. Enlightenment and practice are one.

Ju-ching recognized Dogen's enlightenment and sent him forth as dharma heir to teach Soto Zen in Japan. He encouraged Dogen to avoid cities and politics. He exhorted Dogen to remain pure above all and to practice fiercely. Young Dogen did not follow his teacher's advice at first. Upon his return to the Kennin-ji Monastery in Kyoto, Dogen attempted to gain political acceptance for Soto Zen in that city. Unsuccessful in influencing politics, Dogen withdrew to an outlying province, where he found he could best teach and spread Zen.

Dogen hoped to reform Buddhism in Japan by teaching people to expect nothing, seek nothing, and even hope to gain nothing. All that mattered was the aware meditative practice in everyday life. He encouraged his disciples to give up all attachments and live a simple life devoted to concentrated meditation, which he called zazen (sitting meditation). His instructions for zazen were simple: Find a quiet place, sit on a pillow in a cross-legged position, with your body straight, upright, and two thumbs together at the tips. Keep your breathing steady, while forgetting all attachments. If a wish arises, take note of it and then let it go. As Dogen explained, "This is the art of zazen. Zazen is the dharma gate of great rest and joy" (Dumoulin 1990, 76). Dogen himself dressed in rags—in fact, the dirtier and more ragged the better! Throughout his life, Dogen was a living example of his own message.

Receiving the precepts—the Buddhist rules of conduct and discipline for living an ethical life—was absolutely essential to Dogen. Receiving them meant that disciples accepted and committed themselves to living according to compassionate and selfless guidelines. Following the precepts helped to orient disciples correctly toward themselves and others, opening the door to a meditative life. As Dogen said, "How can you expect to become a buddha if you do not guard against faults and prevent yourself from doing wrong?" (Yokoi 1990, 84). All of the Zen monks who studied with Dogen swore to uphold the Buddhist precepts, and this continues to be an important part of all traditional Zen practice today.

Dogen taught his students that they could devote themselves to Zen Buddhism without supplementing it with other philosophies. Unlike Eisai and Myozen before him, Dogen broke ties with Tendai and Shingon, teaching pure Zen and only Zen. Nothing was necessary other than sitting in meditation.

The cornerstone of Dogen's Zen was to sit in zazen. Dogen taught that practice is enlightenment. We do not practice to become enlightened. We practice as a natural expression of our enlightenment. Dogen explained this in his writings:

In the Buddha-Dharma, practice and realization are identical... Thus, even while one is directed to practice, he is told not to anticipate realization apart from practice, because practice points directly to original realization. As it is already realization in practice, realization is endless; as it is practice in realization, practice is beginningless. (Dumoulin 1990, 79)

ZEN SPREADS THROUGHOUT JAPAN

Dogen founded the Soto line of Zen, the sect of Zen that was devoted to meditation as the supereminent means to enlightenment. The Rinzai line continued to evolve from the students of Eisai. Many Chinese masters, from more than twenty lines of Zen, most under the patronage of shoguns and emperors, emigrated to Japan, helping the Zen movement to grow.

A similar system for the dissemination of Zen that was established in Sung China—Five Mountains, Ten Temples—was instituted in Japan. Both Soto and Rinzai Zen flourished and spread. Rinzai tended to be located in the cities, while Soto temples spread throughout the rural areas.

Zen monks became part of the cultural, social, and economic fabric of Japan. Zen monasteries were centers for the arts and learning, and so Japanese rulers gave the monks the task of educating the people. The government helped organize schools in Zen monasteries to teach people simple academic subjects along with religion. Skills in the arts were also developed and utilized for the purpose of teaching and enhancing Zen. Artists could retreat to the sanctuary of the monastery and develop their talents through the practice of Zen arts.

Chinese Master Wu-men (Mumon in Japanese, 1183-1260) had written out and collected a group of sayings, stories, and question-and-answer dialogues into a koan book, known as the *Mumonkan,* which was brought back to Japan and used as a means of teaching Zen. The koans were used in Rinzai Zen extensively, much like in Sung China. Over time, the phrases indicative of enlightenment that were used by the students in response—phrases of one, two, three, or more words—developed into a network for koan learning.

Fierce rivalry between Soto and Rinzai sects was expressed in heated, often colorful exchanges between them. This statement from Rinzai master Hakuin shows how emotional these interactions became: "I have heard Yung-chiao praised as an outstanding teacher of Soto Zen . . . Don't be lapping at fox slobber like this mess that Yung-chiao spewed before you just now" (Waddell 1994, 23).

Soto practitioners, emphasizing zazen as the central practice, were opposed to Rinzai practitioners, who emphasized koans along with other practices. Soto adherents accused the Rinzai of koan-gazing. Rinzai accused Soto practitioners of wall-gazing.

Despite the back-and-forth quibbling, the differences between Rinzai and Soto were not absolutely clear-cut. Rinzai practitioners used meditation along with koans, and Soto adherents sometimes used koans as a focus for their meditation.

Bankei (1622-1693), a prominent Zen teacher of the Rinzai line bridged the gap between Soto and Rinzai traditions. Even though he was a Rinzai monk, he spoke very little of koan study in his talks, sermons, and dialogues. Instead, sudden enlightenment was his emphasis. Bankei developed the concept of the "unborn mind."

The unborn mind is empty of content—it is the original primordial nature of the mind, the True Self. For example, if you see a car driving toward you on a road, you immediately jump out of the way. It doesn't matter if you are rich or poor, man or woman, your reaction is the same. This is the unborn mind—reacting immediately without thought. Once oriented toward it, the student of Zen is on the Path.

HAKUIN, JAPAN'S MOST INFLUENTIAL RINZAI MASTER

Hakuin (1685-1768), is one of Japan's greatest Zen masters. Although he spent most of his life in a small temple located in his home village, his influence was felt throughout Japan—and now in the West.

Born in the farming village of Hara, near the base of Mount Fuji, Hakuin entered the monkhood as a teenager. He had his head shaved at the village temple, Shoin-ji, under the monk Tanrei. It was Tanrei who gave him the Buddhist name Ekaku. After four years of study at this temple, Hakuin was given permission to develop his understanding by traveling around. He visited many temples, learning from both Soto and Rinzai masters, until he found the mountain hermitage of Shoju.

Hakuin wrote that he wandered throughout the countryside, among the mountains and rivers of Japan, until deep within the forest of Narasawa he found a tiny mountain hermitage. It was here that Master Shoju, also known as Shoju Etan (1642-1721), resided. This action-oriented, dynamic Zen master communicated the Zen spirit to Hakuin. At the age of twenty-four Hakuin had his first enlightenment. But he did not stop there. He continued to deepen his insight.

Hakuin's father became ill and asked that his son return to the village to help him. The dutiful son returned and became the abbot of the Shoin-ji temple. The building was in such bad repair that, Hakuin wrote, he needed to wear a raincoat inside. He remained in the village, caring for his father, and continued to revere and watch over his family even after his father died. He resided in the tiny village temple for fifty years, practicing Zen, immersing himself in study, and deepening his enlightenment.

Students began to come to Hakuin's temple to learn. At first, Hakuin taught reluctantly, for he felt he had not yet been able to integrate enlightenment into his everyday life. But finally he had a pivotal enlightenment experience, and it changed him. His doubts dissolved and he felt completely liberated in all aspects of his life.

Now Hakuin directed his energies to helping others achieve enlightenment. Ultimately, he sought to influence society for its betterment. His fervent zeal and passionate commitment to Zen meditation drew followers from all over Japan. Students flocked to the village for his teaching and influence, often camping out on the temple grounds.

Not only did Hakuin teach Zen, but he also wrote over fifty works, ranging from complex discourses and commentaries to simple songs and chants, clearly explaining Zen. He also created thousands of ink paintings and calligraphy. He painted with the bold, simple techniques typical of Zen painting. Hakuin's work and life are a true example of the enlightened experience.

Hakuin revitalized and reorganized the koan system, and it is said he created one of the most widely known koans:"What is the sound of one hand clapping?" Along with his disciple Gasan Jito (1727-1797) and later heirs Inzan Ien (1751-1814) and Takuju Kosen (1760-1833), Hakuin organized the vast body of koans into a coherent system for study and analysis. His disciples continued the hierarchical structuring of koans and developed categories of formal acceptable answers. One-, two-, and three-word phrases were also cataloged. Hakuin's system included acceptable capping phrases, *jakujo,* for the koan solutions.

Hakuin's system of division into categories used the Five Ranks, a time-honored and accepted set of symbolic concepts that permitted the openness required in Zen constructs while granting a hierarchical image to locate and assess the student's progress on the path. Paradoxically, the Five Ranks was originated by Tosan, one of the two founders of Soto Zen! Hakuin incorporated the Five Ranks system into his own teaching.

Hakuin lived a long and productive life—dying at the age of eighty-three. He was zealous, passionate, and evangelistic, open to whoever would come, and remained a dominating figure in Zen for all time. Most lines of Rinzai trace their lineage through Hakuin. His system of division of the koans into the Five Ranks still stands, monumental in its organizational hierarchy. By following this structure, Zen can be communicated through generations while remaining true to the early spirit first expressed by the Chinese Patriarchs.

Hakuin's Message

Hakuin's writings were forceful, and his teachings were passionate and persuasive. He often told his students, "There's no doubt about it, Zen is a formidable undertaking" (Waddell 1994, 72).

He spoke to the ordinary person rather than just scholars and academicians, exhorting all practitioners to committed, genuine, effortful practice. Anyone could become enlightened with enough effort. Hakuin encouraged his disciples:

> *But once someone vows to achieve enlightenment, no matter what hardships he may face, even if it takes him 30 or 40 years of arduous effort, he should without fail achieve his goal and reach the ground of awakening that was realized and confirmed by the Zen Patriarchs before him. (Waddell 1994, 94)*

Hakuin urged his listeners to try hard to penetrate their true nature through discovery of the meaning of koans, to seek enlightenment. He encouraged faith, brought about doubt, and urged all to strive tenaciously for enlightenment. Hakuin explained what it took to do Zen:

> *Hence a priest of former times, Kao-feng Yuan-miao said, "A person who commits himself to the practice of Zen must be equipped with three essentials: A great root of faith, a great ball of doubt, a great tenacity of purpose. Lacking any one of them he is like a tripod with only two legs." (Waddell 1994, 62)*

Hakuin's lectures and writings were often polemical. He criticized individuals as representatives of faults in practice in order to show, by vivid contrast, the Way.

Though he permitted other forms of Buddhism, he considered zazen superior, more direct, and more genuine than all other ways.

Hakuin's message is an optimistic one: People have everything they need, here and now, to be enlightened and free. Paradise is now, here. We must wake up and live in it, not seek it outside, turning away through other practices. His approach involved both sudden enlightenment through breakthroughs and continual searching, ever onward toward deeper and deeper enlightenment. The Way Hakuin showed has become a central part of Rinzai Zen.

TRANSITIONS

By the eighteenth and early nineteenth centuries, Zen had become an important and accepted part of mainstream Japanese culture. The Tokugawa Shogunate government embraced Buddhism and set up an institutional structure for administration that incorporated each temple into a hierarchy so that branch temples were under the main temples, with each level responsible for the one beneath. Hakuin's temple, a branch temple of a branch temple, was part of this system, vital to the social fabric of Japan in its tiny way. The number of Buddhist temples in Japan increased from 13,037 in the Kamakura (1185-1333) era to 469,934 during Tokugawa rule (1600-1868) (Kitagawa 1966, 160).

Hakuin Zen was carried forth in direct lineage from Hakuin using the step-wise presentations of koans to help practitioners climb a hierarchical ladder to deeper and deeper enlightenment. Meanwhile, Soto Zen monasteries continued to educate the masses not only in Zen but also in basic academic subjects. By the turn of the twentieth century, the national agenda for education became broader and included Western methods. Soto schools were closed and replaced with the modern school system that exists in Japan today.

The interplay between Soto and Rinzai continued during Japan's long feudal era. After the gradual breakdown during the Meiji period (1868–1912) of Japan's feudal structure, the restoration of the emperor and formation of a centralized government brought revitalization of Zen as a national treasure and resource. Zen was combined with indigenous Shintoism and Confucianism, which had long been integrated into Japanese society.

CHAPTER 4

Zen Enters the Modern Age

*Priests of the future, it may be, will learn not only to preside at the Eucharist
but to lead the faithful in meditation, after the manner of an Eastern guru.*
—Graham 1974, 123

ZEN IS BROUGHT TO THE WEST

Daisetsu Teitaro Suzuki (1870-1966), a Japanese practitioner and teacher
of Zen, had a profound influence on the introduction of Zen to the West.

Suzuki visited the West initially in 1893 as a young man of twenty-three
to translate for his teacher, Shaku Soyen (1859-1919), during the
first World Parliament of Religion, held in Chicago. This was the first time
Zen Buddhism had ever been presented to Westerners. Paul Carus, a publisher
at the conference, was so impressed with the Eastern perspective that he
decided to publish English translations of a number of Eastern texts. Shaku
Soyen recommended Suzuki for the job of translator. In the end,
Suzuki stayed in the United States for ten years, living at Paul Carus's house,

translating a number of books and sutras in the areas of Taoism, Buddhism, and eventually Zen.

Shaku Soyen returned to the United States in 1905 at the invitation of Mrs. Alexander Russell of San Francisco to give talks on Zen for the benefit of her friends. Suzuki again acted as Soyen's translator as he lectured throughout northern and southern California. They visited the Japanese consulate and Buddhist temples until the spring, when Soyen was invited to the East Coast, where he gave lectures in New York, Philadelphia, and Boston. He spoke in Japanese and Suzuki interpreted and explained what he meant. Soyen continued on to Europe, but without Suzuki, who returned to his translating work.

Suzuki finished his work for Paul Carus and went back to Japan. He taught English at several universities and continued translating Buddhist works. He married Beatrice Erskine Lane, an American, in 1911. In 1921, he was offered the position of professor of Buddhist studies at Otani University and began publishing a journal entitled *The Eastern Buddhist*. He did not begin writing books on Zen in English until his middle years, but continued to write prolifically on the subject for over four decades. He was awarded a doctorate in literature from Otani University at the age of sixty-three. Suzuki lectured throughout the world, including China, England, and Europe. In the United States, he spoke at a number of American universities, among them Claremont College, Princeton, Harvard, Chicago, Yale, Cornell, Northwestern, and Wesleyan, and taught at Columbia for a number of years.

Suzuki continued along the path that he had blazed, bridging East and West, articulating the concepts of Zen, Mahayana Buddhism, and Taoist thought. The majority of his more than 125 books and articles covered aspects of Rinzai Zen teachings and practice, the interrelationships of Zen with culture, and even a study of the thought of the German mystic, Meister Eckhart, in relationship to Zen. His frame of reference was that of Rinzai Zen, but much of what he wrote applied to Soto practitioners as well, since both schools are related to the early classical masters through Hui-neng. Suzuki lived a long and productive life, influencing many later Zen writers in both the United States and Europe.

Suzuki made it his life's work to clarify the Zen Way, relating it intelligently to Western readers and students through traditional stories, koans, and historical accounts, as well as philosophical conceptualizations that compared it to Western counterparts. His work contributed greatly to the acceptance and comprehension of Zen in the West.

SUZUKI'S IDEAS ABOUT ZEN

Suzuki described the Zen life clearly and carefully in his prolific writings. He detailed meanings that were significant to understanding Zen by articulately expressing key terms, principles, and actions based on these principles.

Suzuki thought systematic methods could be limiting; he believed the Zen master should teach the student according to the student's individual needs. The spectrum of possible interchanges between student and teacher is practically infinite, limited only by needs, personalities, and circumstances. The Zen master seeks to awaken the student to realization of enlightenment, the true self, given in the experience of satori. Suzuki described how this can be brought about through stories, koans, and even the daily customs, rituals, and activities of the monks. He explained how Zen can be expressed in a virtuous and ethical lifestyle, which he called "secret virtue" (D.T. Suzuki 1994, 58), on doing the deed for its own sake without thought of reciprocity. The action of giving is an expression of sunyata, of emptiness. No expectation of response is held. The task is there to be done. Suzuki considered this parallel to Christian good works, such as Mother Teresa's attending to those for whom no one else would care.

Suzuki accepted and followed Hui-neng's position on instant enlightenment and pointed out how Zen methods attempt to bring this about.

He analyzed experience in terms of simple categories in order to differentiate one mode of mental functioning from another.

One of Suzuki's intriguing explanatory constructs was the unconscious mind. Suzuki believed enlightened mental functioning was unconscious, yet intelligent and attuned. By unconscious he meant nonconscious, prajna, a wiser intuitive capacity that is attuned to the nature of people and things. Conscious reasoning and analytical thought could not bring enlightenment (see Chapter 6): "The highest act of our consciousness is indeed to penetrate through all the conceptual deposits and read the bedrock of prajna: the unconscious" (Suzuki 1972, 154).

True to Zen, Suzuki is a paradox: a scholar with an academic background and training, using the intellect to express the nonintellectual, the experiential. He used a university setting to communicate Zen's intuitive understandings to vast numbers of people, concepts to express the nonconceptual.

Suzuki wrote about many of the themes of Zen. He addressed the issue of defining what Zen is. In this way he helped communicate its principles.

ZEN MASTERS IN THE WEST

Following D. T. Suzuki, a number of Zen masters came from Japan to teach Zen to the West. Shunryu Suzuki (1905-1971), a renowned Soto Zen monk and teacher, first came to the United States for a visit in 1958. When he saw how sincerely interested Americans were in learning Zen, he decided to settle in San Francisco. His original meditation group grew to three locations devoted to teaching Zen, including the San Francisco Zen Center.

Shunryu Suzuki had a quiet, modest disposition, meditatively aware, moment to moment. He told his students: "If you continue this simple practice every day, you will obtain some wonderful power. Before you attain it, it is something wonderful, but after you attain it, it is nothing special" (S. Suzuki 1979, 46).

He called practice a "single-hearted effort" and recommended that even if you feel confused or find it difficult to stop your mind from racing, you should continue to sit for meditation. "In continuous practice, under a succession of agreeable and disagreeable situations, you will realize the marrow of Zen and acquire its true strength" (S. Suzuki 1979, 40).

Korean Zen master Seung Sahn (b. 1927) came to Providence, Rhode Island, in 1972. He inspired a number of Brown University students who helped him to found the Providence Zen Center, now part of the Kwan Um School of Zen, formed in 1983. His Korean Zen has since spread throughout the United States and Europe.

Seung Sahn developed a way of teaching Americans that uses straightforward language to crystalize Zen's meaning. He advises his students to "only go straight" and develop "don't-know mind." Here he explains:

How do you understand your true self? What are you? Do you know? If you don't know, only go straight—don't know. Then this don't know mind cuts off all thinking, and your only-me situation, only-me condition, and only-me opinion disappear. Then your correct situation, correct condition, and correct opinion appear—very simple. (Seung Sahn 1992, 12)

ZEN INTEGRATES WITH WESTERN TRADITIONS

If we only knew in the Western world how much of our lives actually contain within them the seeds of Zen. Unfortunately, many of us spend our lives denying this fact and, as a result, we deny an important part of ourselves.
—*Hall 1983, 87*

Today, Zen is finding a place throughout the United States and Europe. There are many Zen centers where people can participate at various levels of involvement, from a onetime weekend seminar to daily meditation sessions.

Zen can be practiced in conjunction with other beliefs and religions, as it is in the East. In Japan, Korea, and China, people often adhered to Buddhism, Confucianism, and Taoism at the same time. The saying was "Three practices, One Way."

Here in the West, Zen can creatively intertwine with the Judeo-Christian tradition. Roman Catholic monks at the Abbey of Gethsemani hold regular meditation sessions with Zen monks. These Catholic monks have been living with sincere simplicity since the order was founded in 1098. In the twentieth century, they find that Zen meditation enhances their own practice.

Brother Benjamin of the Abbey of Gethsemani explained the commonality with Zen:

> Dae Soen Sa Nim's joy, his energy, his direct teaching going to the heart of the matter, resonate in our Cistercian monastic tradition....Getting up at 3am we chant the psalms in choir. Why do we do this? If you ask the Zen master he says, "Just sing. Just chant." There is no need to check the performance. (Seung Sahn 1992, xxvi)

More and more, meditation is being meaningfully integrated into the many facets of daily life, helping different types of people live with more awareness and sensitivity. The Path is open to all.

> The great path has no gates,
> Thousands of roads enter it,
> When one passes through this gateless gate
> He walks freely between heaven and earth. (Mumonkan in Reps 1994, 114)

Zen Themes

Zen concepts
Empty yet not
Wordless wisdom
Beyond all thought
— C. Alexander Simpkins

Themes and concepts are often used to help understand a subject. For Zen, concepts can point to the Way, but they are never the Path itself. As you read Part II, consider these concepts as guidelines to turn you in the right direction, away from superficial thinking, back toward your deeper, true nature as found in the meditative awareness of direct experience. Like a compass guiding you through unchartered waters, these themes will help you steer your ship as you venture on your journey toward enlightenment.

CHAPTER 5

Beyond Words and Objects
to Self-Awakening

A special tradition outside the scriptures No dependence upon
words or letters. Direct pointing at the soul of man Seeing into
one's nature and the attainment of buddhahood.
—Bodhidharma (Simpkins and Simpkins 1996, 21)

This famous statement epitomizes Zen: self-awakening beyond words. Direct
pointing to one's true nature is a nonconceptual experience that goes straight
to the core, engaging intuitive knowing rather than interpretive analysis.

Yet the many thousands of volumes written through the ages about Zen
attest to the fact that words and concepts do have a place. Although Zen
masters often seem to denigrate words, properly used words and concepts are
a valuable tool in Zen. Rinzai master Ta-hui explains:

There are two forms of error now prevailing among followers of Zen, laymen as well as monks. The one thinks that there are wonderful things hidden in words and phrases, and those who hold this view try to learn many words and phrases. The second goes to the other extreme, forgetting that words are the pointing finger, showing one where to locate the moon... Only when these two erroneous views are done away with is there a chance for real advancement in the mastery of Zen. (D. T, Suzuki 1994, 79)

In Western culture we take for granted that language corresponds to objects in the real world. A noun correlates to an object, and an object relates to descriptive words. For example the noun "book" corresponds to this book you hold in your hands. Zen has a different perspective. In Zen, words are used as maps that point to an area, but they are only a map, an abstraction. Zen Buddhists state clearly that words themselves should not be confused with what they point to, the territory. In fact, reliance on words and concepts is often intimately linked with our problems, according to Zen Buddhism. People can become entangled in a confusing web of abstractions. Interpreting through language is transitory and relative; words separate us from the world. Experiencing directly returns us to the true nature of life, reality, and ourselves.

This concept is illustrated in the following koan story. Fa-yen (885-958) was the Chinese Zen master of one of the Five Houses of Zen (House of Fa-yen) that thrived during the latter half of the T'ang dynasty. At the time of this story Fa-yen lived alone at a small country temple. Four traveling monks who were passing through asked if they could rest in his yard and build a fire. Fa-yen agreed. As they began gathering firewood, he overheard them arguing about the difference between the subjective and objective. Fa-yen saw an opportunity to teach them Zen, and asked, "Do you see the big stone over there? Is it inside or outside your mind?"

One of the monks answered, "If you look at this from the Buddhist perspective, since Buddhist philosophy states that ultimately everything we perceive derives from the mind, I would have to say that this stone is an objectification of my mind."

"Well, then, your head must weigh a lot if you are carrying this heavy stone with you!" answered Fa-yen, humorously.

POINTING THE WAY

How does Zen use language to help students find their way? Instead of instructing didactically, Zen masters guide students indirectly, through action, stories, and even silence. The original Zen patriarchs and their dharma heirs created special teaching aids communicated in Zen's characteristic manner. Like a boat that carries you across a river, descriptive language can bring you to the shore. But then you must leave the boat behind and venture into the wilderness on foot. For centuries, koan collections like the *Hekiganroku* and *Mumonkan* have been used as aids to transmit to students, no matter where or when they were learning, the primary teachings of the original Chinese Ch'an Patriarchs.

Teaching stories work on many levels. The first reading of a Zen story can offer a view through imagination's window of the Zen experience. Visualize a scene from the story of Mahakasyapa smiling as Buddha raised a flower in front of his assembly of disciples—the first transmission (see page 5). Mind-to-mind transmission was shared between the two men. While reading this story, you may visualize the scene in your own mind. Perhaps you picture a large group of people dressed in orange robes, sitting cross-legged on the ground, facing one man who is holding a flower, silent, smiling. You look around the group and see serious expressions on all the faces except one person, and that person, too, is smiling.

If you set aside rational analysis, this scene might remind you of a personal memory, a time in your life when you felt a sudden flash of understanding about a subject you were being taught. Perhaps the teacher said or did something that made the instruction suddenly clear. The insight springs from your intuition. You get a glimpse of the inner mind of the teacher and this inspires your own understanding. Mind-to-mind transmission has taken place, similar to Zen, on a smaller scale.

THE USE OF KOANS

Rinzai Zen developed the koan system to help students find and develop the awakened awareness that is called enlightenment. The koan tradition, popularized by Ta-hui in China and refined by Hakuin and his disciples in Japan, allowed Zen to continue to be transmitted from the mind of the original Patriarchs and T'ang masters to students of the present day. Even Soto Zen, with its emphasis on zazen meditation, draws from stories of Zen masters, often given by masters to their students during their dharma talks. D. T. Suzuki explains the importance of koans:

> The idea is to unfold the Zen psychology in the mind of the uninitiated and to reproduce the state of consciousness of which these [koan] statements are the expression. That is to say, when the koans are understood, the master's state of mind is understood, which is satori and without which Zen is a sealed book. (D. T. Suzuki 1994, 81)

Ruth Fuller Sasaki was one of the first Western women to become involved in Zen. She founded the First Zen Institute of America in New York City in 1930, continuing the Rinzai tradition that used koans extensively. She explained:

The koan is not a conundrum to be solved by a nimble wit. It is not a verbal psychiatric device for shocking the disintegrated ego of a student into some kind of stability. Nor, in my opinion, is it ever a paradoxical statement except to those who view it from outside. When the koan is resolved it is realized to be a simple and clear statement made from the state of consciousness which it has helped to awaken. (Sasaki and Miura 1965, xi)

Here is a typical koan story from the *Mumonkan,* Case 24. A monk asked Fuketsu (896-973), one of Lin-chi's dharma heirs, "Without words and without no-words, can you tell me of enlightenment?" Fuketsu replied, "I cannot forget springtime in Konan where the birds sing and how fragrant the flowers!"

The literature of Zen is filled with the koan stories of many Zen masters, and students today share in these experiences much like the original students did. Explanations are not given. Instead, students are asked to meditate on the story carefully without analyzing or reverting to rational thinking. The story itself offers an opportunity for experience beyond the usual words.

Learning in Zen is nonconceptual, direct, and difficult to articulate. Concepts, labels, and rational judgments interfere with spontaneous, enlightened action. Japanese Zen master Kosen (1816-1892) confronted this one day at his temple.

A large carved wooden sign hangs in front of the Obaku (Huang-Po) temple in Kyoto. It reads: "The First Principle." Master Kosen drew the template for the letters that he planned to have carved by artisans. A student watched as he drew the letters.

"That is not very good," said the student as he perused Kosen's work.

Kosen tried again. "What about this one?" asked Kosen.

"Worse than the last one!" answered the student.

Kosen continued to write, over and over, page after page, but the student criticized every one. Finally, the disciple excused himself for a moment to go inside, leaving Kosen alone. Kosen thought to himself, "Here is my opportunity!" With that, he wrote swiftly and surely, his mind clear of all judgments.

When the student returned, all he could say was, "Perfect!"

Zen frees us from distracting, limiting concepts that inhibit and constrain us, making us self-conscious and alienated from our deeper nature. Without these restrictions to hold us back, everything becomes possible.

"Penetrating" the koan is the student's task. He is to think about it day and night, like a person deprived of liquid on a hot summer day thinks only of water.

Nan-ch'uan (Nansen in Japanese, 748-835) was a direct student of Ma-tsu and the subject of several koans. In Case 27 of the *Mumonkan*—"It Is Not Mind, It Is Not Buddha, It Is Not Things"—a monk asked Nan-ch'uan, "Are there any teachings that have not been taught before?"

Nan-ch'uan answered, "Yes."

"Well, what is this truth that has not been preached?" asked the monk.

"It is not mind, it is not Buddha, it is not things," answered Nan-ch'uan.

By wrestling with the same dilemmas that the early masters offered to their disciples, contemporary students of Zen go through experiences similar to their historical counterparts. At first students attempt to fall back on their usual modes of reasoning, as if solving a rational puzzle. This leads nowhere, which throws students into an overwhelming feeling of doubt of all that has been known before. But this is exactly what the koan is supposed to do, to shake people out of the complacency of ordinary thinking. As students continue to focus on the koan, in time, they break through to the unconscious, which C. G. Jung called "great liberation" (Dumoulin 1988, 254).

WORDLESS POINTING: SHOUTS AND HITS

Chinese Zen masters Ma-tsu and Lin-chi often resorted to shouting or hitting in response to students' questions. This created tension in the students, since they never knew when they might receive a smack from the master. The purpose, however, was not to terrorize the students but to give them a direct, wordless, nonconceptual experience. If you think about a time you were surprised by something—for example, a ball thrown at you unexpectedly—you probably extended your arms and caught it without thinking. Bankei referred to this as the Unborn Mind. This is the kind of nonrational awareness that Zen helps us awaken. Frequently, students who were struck by Lin-chi's stick discovered sudden enlightenment.

Here is a typical exchange between Lin-chi and a student.

The Master said to a nun, "Well come, or ill come?
The nun gave a shout.
The Master picked up his stick and said, "Speak then, speak!"
The nun shouted once more.
The Master struck her. (Watson 1993, 99)

Like any teaching device, koans, shouting, and strikes with the stick are not the awareness itself. They are aids to engage students toward awakening. Words can point to the experience, like the finger pointing to the moon, but they cannot become the experience itself. (See Chapter 9 to experiment with koans.) When you meditate on koans, do not mistake the means for the end ... or the beginning. Employ them as a useful vehicle to help you get to the other shore.

FOLLOWING THE PATH

There are several paths to Zen awakening propounded by different sects of Zen. Although all Zen Buddhists accept that Mind is the Buddha, that the wisdom found in pure awareness is already within you, there are differences in how to realize this. Rinzai practitioners believe that people have barriers that must be broken through with rigorous and absolute devotion. To help guide students along the journey, Rinzai Zen uses koans that present steps to climb.

Students are given a koan when they first enter the monastery and are told to work on it. Each day they see the teacher for a short session, called dokusan. During this brief encounter the student tells the master what he or she thinks the koan is expressing. The master can tell by the answer whether the student is progressing on the Path. As soon as the student masters one koan, a new one is given. Rinzai schools present five ranks, or levels, of koans. After the Fifth Rank (Mu) is penetrated, some Rinzai schools, such as Zen Mountain Monastery in New York, present students with the precepts, the moral and ethical teachings of Buddha, treating them like a koan. Students meditate on the precepts to learn how to truly live enlightenment, acting ethically each moment.

Soto Zen does not encourage practitioners to discover awakened awareness in this way. They believe that sitting in zazen only (shikantaza) is the most direct path to take. Koans are a means of focusing attention while sitting in meditation. Sitting need not mean literally sitting down. Standing, walking, and working are not any different in offering opportunities to enter the Way. Thus, the path is clear. Dogen's single-minded commitment to zazen was an inspiration to countless generations who continue to follow Dogen's example. Soto monks are just as committed as the Rinzai monks, but their daily routines are somewhat different. Meditation and work are the mainstays of life at Soto Zen monasteries, with little use of koans.

The journey of discovery has been traveled for centuries. Deep, clear awareness opens a new vista of experience, transforming the person. As Bodhidharma said, "The opening of the inner eye is the door of the Great Vehicle" (Pine 1989, 49). Everything is different and yet nothing is different. This is the paradox of enlightenment.

CHAPTER 6

Emptiness: Not Even Nothing Exists

*When your spirit is not in the least clouded, when the clouds of
bewilderment clear away, there is the true void.*
—(Musashi 1974, 95)

Emptiness is fundamental to Zen, reaching back to the enlightenment of
Buddha. The stories, traditions, customs, and accounts of exchanges with
masters may be beautiful and mysterious at times, but, like a handcrafted box,
their usefulness is in their emptiness. The interrelationship of the parts of Zen
form to make emptiness. One of the sutras that points to this, the Heart Sutra,
states: "Form is emptiness, emptiness is form."

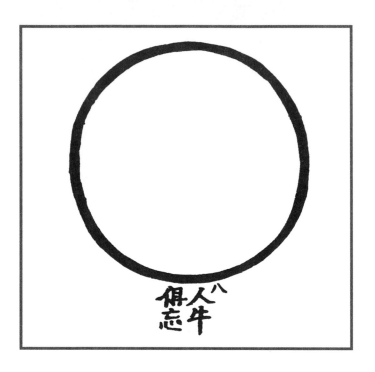

DISCOVERY OF NOTHINGNESS

The concept of "nothing" had been noticed by Eastern philosophy for thousands of years, but like dark holes in space, it was not understood. Early mathematicians did not have a term for it. They knew that the absence of any quantity was present, but they were at a loss as to what it was. They could not account for it.

The Hindus were the first to recognize zero, which they called sunya, meaning void or empty. Once they discovered sunya, mathematics as we know it today became possible. All computations were revolutionized by the recognition that "nothing" was "something." Suddenly, zero existed. Then came the midpoint on the arithmetical number line: minus one, zero, plus one. Number systems developed from this, but the important evolutionary jump was the discovery of nothingness.

> *Discovery of the zero marks the decisive stage in a process of development without which we cannot imagine the progress of modern mathematics, science, and technology. The zero freed human intelligence from the counting board that held it prisoner for thousands of years, eliminating all ambiguity in the written expression of numbers, revolutionized the art of reckoning, and made it accessible to everyone. (Ifrah, 1987, 433)*

Binary arithmetic, based on one and zero, has made computers possible. Without "nothingness," what is cannot be.

Mahayana Buddhism's emptiness, known as sunyata, was the springboard for Zen. If originally "not a thing is" (Ma-tsu), then there is no reason to objectify or make an object of what we perceive or know. Words are not used as concepts in Zen. We can expand this understanding when we realize that objects are interrelated to our perceptions of them. The experience of perception is primary.

EMPTINESS AS PROCESS

In Zen, emptiness is not a concept or goal, nor is it an ultimate state. This is different from the Western scientific concept that defines emptiness as a state, a vacuum consisting of the absence of molecules. For Zen Buddhists, emptiness is a process, a continuum, always in flux. The founder of Gestalt therapy, Fritz Perls, noted that the void implies no-thingness, only process. Perls believed the void was a source of creativity and therapeutic change (Perls 1969, 57).

Zen masters discourage immersion in any kind of empty state. Instead, they help students to discover the process. Hakuin strongly urged students of Zen not to get stuck in the swamp of nothingness. When Yamaoka Tesshu (1836-1888) was a young Zen student, he searched for enlightenment by visiting one Zen master after another. He tried to show each teacher that he knew a great deal about Buddhism. Talking with Master Dokuon of Shokoku he said, "I know that the mind, the Buddha, all beings, and everything in the world does not exist. In fact, the nature of all things is emptiness."

Dokuon watched the young student silently, calmly smoking. Without warning, he lifted his bamboo stick and struck Tesshu.

Tesshu felt himself fill with anger.

Then Dokuon said, "If nothing exists, where did that anger come from?"

Everyday life must continue as always. Tesshu needed to learn to let go of even the concept of nothing as a thing. Instead of trying to make yourself nothing, make nothing your true self. If you get too caught up in trying to be nothing, you are making just as big a mistake as those who are trying to be something. Do not try to be nothing or something; meditate to discover enlightenment.

NO SELF, NO OTHER

According to Buddhist thinking, the idea that we have a separate self is an illusion. There is no external individual being apart from interaction with the world. Each of us has individual perceptions, consciousness, and sensations. All of these experiences are ongoing as we go through life. Yet Buddhists believe that it is a mistake to gather all of these experiences into a fixed concept of a "self." This is a false inference, an unfounded leap in logic. The collection of these experiences is all you can really be certain of. Experiencing takes place. Nothing more. We cannot necessarily conclude anything further. René Descartes's famous conclusion does not necessarily follow. Instead of his statement "I think, therefore I am," Zen Buddhists would say "I think I am, therefore I appear." Our concept of ourselves is really just a function of how we experience and how others experience us. Zen Buddhists hold that the individual self is actually an expression of the True Self, which is deeply spiritual and One with all things. Concepts of self and self-nature obscure direct experience. Zen Buddhists encourage us to let go of these confusions.

According to social psychology, the concept of self is a result of interactions with significant other people and their interactions with you. But if the concept of self is an illusion, then so too is the concept of other; no-self in Zen also means no-other. There is no self, there is no other—all disappear in the Oneness. When Emperor Wu asked Bodhidharma, "Who is this standing before me?" and Bodhidharma answered, "I do not know," he was replying sincerely. He really did not know. Form is emptiness, including ourselves and other people. Bodhidharma was as puzzled as Emperor Wu.

Applying this logic, if we hurt another we only hurt ourselves. There is no one apart from ourselves. This is Zen's solution to many of the social conflicts people have. We need not try to empathize or identify with other people. When we open our awareness to Zen emptiness, we realize we are already part of others as they are part of us. We cannot separate ourselves from others. We are inseparably at one with our social world.

The Zen Unconscious

Emptiness is expressed naturally in the Zen unconscious. The unconscious, as D. T. Suzuki uses the term, does not refer to a personal unconscious. Since we have no fixed self, we cannot have a single, separate unconscious either. Unconscious awareness is known as absolute prajna, or wisdom. Thus, the Zen unconscious is the source for potential:

> *The Zen masters, ultimately deriving their philosophy from the Buddhist doctrine of sunyata and prajna, describe the unconscious in terms of life, that is, of birth and death, which is no-birth-and-death . . . For the unconscious then permits its privileged disciples, masters of the arts, to have glimpses of its infinite possibilities. (D. T. Suzuki 1973, 193)*

The Zen unconscious is brought about by letting go of conscious concerns and intent through no-mindedness: "To have thoughts as though not having them [Hui-neng], this evidently means to be conscious of the Unconscious or to find the Unconscious in consciousness" (D. T. Suzuki 1972, 126).

Zen ascribes no reality, in an absolute sense, to thoughts and perceptions from individual minds. In a relative sense, there may be appearances, but they are merely an outer manifestation.

The conditions of the physical world and the senses may project the image of an apparent object, but no object is actually present. It is like a mirage of water on an expanse of sunny highway. No water is actually there, merely its realistic appearance due to light bending on the hot road. Similarly, the world that we experience is a function of perceptual conditions.

Consciousness makes it seem to exist.

Koans, sitting in meditation, and other practices in which Zen adherents engage reinstate the unconscious. According to Zen, unconscious functioning offers unlimited potential and is more attuned to reality.

CHAPTER 7

Ethics Are Expressed in Correct Living

It is said that there were eighty-four thousand virtues of perfection practised by all Bodhisattvas, but they are no more than so many leaves and branches growing from the one stem of pure-heartedness.
—Soyen 1987, 78

ETHICS COME FROM EMPTINESS

It would seem paradoxical that Zen, which holds nothing sacred, can be ethical. But an ethical position is fundamental to Zen, implicit in the standpoint of emptiness and unity. Since the ultimate ethical stand of Zen is expressed in action, there is no inconsistency between the quietistic monastic life of some monks and the activist life of others. Both forms of action can be ethical. Both are valid.

In the West, we tend to think of ethics from the standpoint of Aristotle: There is good and evil, based on the distinction between whether a thing is or is not. Zen proposes that we can experience our self and our world from a perspective apart from the polarity of good and evil. This perspective results in a committed ethical position based on nothing: emptiness, as will become clear.

Zen draws its ethical perspective from Mahayana Buddhist philosophy, which believes objective reality is not a distinct, unchallengeable certainty. Indeed, nothing can be ascertained from an examination of what is existing, to prove its existence. The world and a separate, individual self may seem convincingly real, given by the nature of matter and the senses, but ultimately both are merely illusions Nothing exists and yet all things exist simultaneously.

Ethics Come from Oneness

Zen Buddhists do not distinguish between the individual self and the external world in the ultimate sense. We are not separate or separable from the world. We are a part of it. Furthermore, we cannot separate ourselves from our actions or their consequences. Practice and enlightenment are One, and, therefore, our actions are another opportunity to experience the buddha mind.

Actions flow from the standpoint of Oneness. Any harm done is not only harming another; it is also harming you. The wise response is compassion. This means that a wholehearted embrace of goodness is possible in this world. The ethical position of Zen permits an ultimate optimism based on letting go of all illusion.

We tend to expect that fair actions are reciprocal. We expect the recipro-cation of the Golden Rule: Do unto others as you would have them do unto you. Zen bases its ethical position on different grounds. Reciprocity is not required because we cannot separate ourselves from the other, our actions, or their consequences. We may hope for proper treatment in return as a natural expression of our Oneness with the true nature or true self, but it is not the basis for our own actions. Actions are performed for their own sake, not because of outside pressure. D. T. Suzuki refers to this as secret virtue. The Zen monk performs good actions as devotion simply to do them. The personal ego is not important. Good behavior flows from giving oneself fully to the needs of the situation. Reciprocity takes care of itself; first, perform the beneficial service.

> *Not to let your left hand know what your right hand does—this is known in the Zendo life as practicing "secret virtue." It is also the spirit of service. Secret virtue is the deed done for its own sake, not looking for any form of compensation anywhere, neither in heaven nor on earth. (D. T. Suzuki 1994, 58)*

Zen and Christian Ethics Compared

Dom Aelred Graham, a Catholic Benedictine monk, traveled to Asia in 1968 looking for common ground between Eastern religions and Christianity. Among his many dialogues and interviews, he spoke with Soto Zen master Fujaimoto Roshi on the question of ethics. Their discussion clearly shows that Zen defines ethics very differently from Christian religions, and yet Zen monks consistently behave ethically, just as Christian monks do. Although the basis for ethics differs, the practice of ethics is the same.

> *A. G.: I'd like to raise a question on conduct, ethics. Christians try to conform their conduct to some external law given by God or given by the church. That cannot be, of course, in Buddhism. How in practice do Buddhists know what is the right thing or the wrong thing to do? What is their rule of action in everyday life so that they know what to do?*

F.R.: The concept of ethics does not come into Buddhism. What we talk about is always Enlightenment. If one is enlightened, everything he does is good . . . in other words, he lives in the domain where there is no distinction between good and evil. (Graham 1968, 100-101)

This rather shocking statement does not mean what it seems to on the surface. We tend to seek a rule to follow in order to behave ethically. We use an external criterion of what is good. When Buddhists say there is no good and there is no evil, they do not mean that there is no distinction, that anything goes. Buddhists believe that good is not outside of this here and now. No external ideal, no criterion exists. Each thing, each moment is in itself complete and good. Ideals must be made real by living them right now. Now is all there is. Either you are being virtuous now or you are not. If you are not living ethically, there can be no enlightenment. Your life is an expression of enlightenment. Your social interactions are inseparable from enlightenment: All is buddha mind. Fijaimoto Roshi explained this:

We talk about the ideal, and we usually try to accomplish the ideal. But in Zen there is no fixed, specified ideal or goal that we have to reach . . . The goal is infinite . . . The present moment is the goal itself. It is the process, it is the state. In Zen, every moment is here now. Apart from that there is nothing. It is the goal, it is the stage, it is the process, it is the absolute. (Graham 1968, 101)

Zen Buddhists believe that rules of ethics are often based on relativistic norms and standards that may result in varying interpretations of how to behave, depending on cultural conditions, history, and even broader variables like the epoch. This brings about questions of choice and decision. But enlightenment gives a basis for interpretation founded in the absolute, in continuous harmony with enlightenment itself. Behavior should not be guided by an external, relative standard or the ground we stand on is like quicksand. We sink. Actions and conduct flow from an inner basis. The stable ideal, the standard for action, is whether the action is in synchrony with Oneness, with true nature. Unethical or bad behavior flows from disharmony with enlightenment. "To live according to his true nature is the life of the enlightened man, the life of a Buddha. Whatever he does in accordance with his true nature is good" (Graham 1968, 103).

Zen's view of ethics is not apart from the religious experience itself. "Goodness" must be expressed as part of the trueness to nature as they speak of it in Confucianism. In Zen, this moment, as it is, is the intuitive source.

THE VOW TO THE PRECEPTS

Zen does not prescribe in its doctrine what actions to take moment to moment, but Zen monks do take certain vows. All must swear to three vows of Mahayana Buddhism. Hui-neng, the Sixth Patriarch, encouraged his followers to take refuge in precepts he called "the three gems of our essence of mind." These three gems are the three vows:

> *Buddha, which stands for enlightenment*
> *Dharma, which stands for orthodoxy*
> *Sangha [the order], which stands for purity. (Price and Mou-lam 1990, 103)*

He explained that when people take refuge in enlightenment, evil impulses and ideas do not arise. Taking refuge in the dharma keeps people free from cravings, egotism, and arrogance. Letting the mind take refuge in purity, people will not be drawn to the many temptations in the outer environment. By vowing to commit themselves in these ways, practitioners promise to devote themselves to searching for and staying with the Buddhist Way. The nature of these primary precepts does not prescribe how to act or what to do. Rather, the vows are an absolute commitment to enlightenment. From the absolute standpoint of enlightenment, ethical action flows naturally.

CHAPTER 8

Enlightenment Is Wisdom's Fulfillment

I came back into the hall and was about to go to my seat when the whole outlook changed. A broad expanse opened, and the ground appeared as if all caved in . . . As I looked around and up and down, the whole universe with its multitudinous sense-objects now appeared quite different; what was loathsome before, together with ignorance and passions, was now seen to be nothing else but the outflow of my own inmost nature which in itself remained bright, true, and transparent
—Yuan-chou, in Watts 1960, 20.

Many different words are used to describe enlightenment: "One Absolute Thought," sunyata (emptiness), canti (tranquility), clear mind, everyday mind, unconscious, prajna (wisdom), satori, kensho, seeing into one's true nature . . . so many words to describe a wordless experience!

What is it, then, that has so captivated people around the world that they engage in the practice of meditation as their path to a better life? Zen teaches us to sit, calmly breathing, without thinking about anything, keenly aware. In time, we come to a different experience. As Suzuki explains, "It is the privilege of satori to be sitting in the Absolute Present quietly surveying the past and contemplating the future" (Abe 1986, 35). As you come to recognize your potential, discovered through meditating, you experience your own being differently. Feelings of uncertainty and confusion give way to clarity—a Oneness, "Our original inseparability with the universe" (Watts 1960, 86). The first steps, the root of the discovery of something greater, begin with something smaller—turning toward your own mind. Voltaire's famous statement in Candide, "Cultivez votre jardin"—points us in the correct direction.

Zen meditation brings about a unique experience: the stream of thinking quiets, consciousness becomes clear and empty, awareness is moment to moment, fully present. Then, something can happen: enlightenment.

POTENTIAL WITHIN

> *When enlightenment comes*
> *Nothing is there*
> *And so we ask,*
> *Enlightenment is . . . where?*
> —C. Alexander Simpkins

Self-awareness does not come from outside you. When Buddha realized his enlightenment under the bodhi tree, he suddenly knew that the potential for the experience had always been there. He had not known where to look or how to look. Zen Buddhism is an optimistic philosophy in which all people have the capacity for enlightenment latent within. Huang-po expressed this when he said, "All sentient beings are already of one form with Bodhi [enlightenment]" (Blofeld 1994, 144).

This potential often becomes actualized suddenly. Some monks experienced enlightenment after being struck with a stick by their master in response to questions like "What is enlightenment?" or "How do I find it?" All of these cases, and countless others as well, illustrate how enlightenment often comes when it is least expected, surprising the practitioner, opening a clear pathway for emergence of what is already there, in latent form.

Lin-chi said, "Nothing is missing." There is nothing missing, since there is nothing to start with. Zen encourages people to have faith in themselves and not to go looking for something outside of themselves. Enlightenment is a capacity that is already present—a sixth sense. It cannot be gotten from anyone else. Teachers and books can point the way, but the experience is always your own.

PARADISE HERE AND NOW

Many religions promise a better place beyond this world. For Zen, your own efforts in this moment are your best doorway to paradise. Paradise is here and now, not in some other place or time. One of the key doctrines in Zen Buddhism that Dogen expressed clearly was the interpenetration of all things: Everything comes into being altogether; all phenomena are interrelated and interconnected. There is no separation between people, their lives, or their enlightenment. A Zen master was asked how to enter the Path to enlightenment. His answer was a question, "Do you hear the stream?"

"Yes," responded the student.

"Well then, you have found the entrance to the Path!" No aspect of your life—career, family, leisure—is outside of your enlightenment. All are intimately linked. Anything you do can become a place to begin your search for enlightenment, as well as helping you to maintain it. Some people might think, "My life is boring. I long for something better!" Zen discourages this kind of thinking as dualistic, leading you away from enlightenment. Your boredom, when you are fully aware of it and one with it, may be your best pathway to an intuitive leap of understanding.

Long ago in Japan, a shogun asked Zen Master Takuan (1573-1645) how to deal with his boredom. He complained that he spent every day sitting uncomfortably in his office taking care of governmental duties. Takuan composed the following poem in answer:

> *Not twice this day*
> *Inch time foot gem.*
> *This day will not come again.*
> *Each minute is worth a priceless gem. (Reps 1994, 50)*

Live every moment fully, letting each experience receive your equal and full attention. Here and now is where enlightenment can be found; here and now can be your paradise.

NOTHING SPECIAL

Zen Masters have often told their students that enlightenment is nothing special. It is, in the Buddhist sense of the word, empty. Therefore, there is nothing to accomplish, nothing to achieve, nothing to get. A student who had come from Hui-neng's temple was asked what instructions the master had given him. He answered, "According to his instructions, no-tranquilization, no-disturbance, no-sitting, no-meditation—this is the Tathagata's Dhyana [meditation]" (D. T. Suzuki 1972, 35).

Shunryu Suzuki, explained that enlightenment might seem to be something extraordinary, but:

70

For a mother with children, having children is nothing special. That is zazen. So, if you continue this practice, more and more you will acquire something— nothing special, but nevertheless something. You may say, "universal nature" or "Buddha nature" or "enlightenment." You may call it many names, but for the person who has it, it is nothing, and it is something. (S. Suzuki 1979, 48)

Even though Zen students are seriously devoted to discovering enlightenment, it cannot be sought after. No particular outcome or effect should be expected. This seems paradoxical for our modern, goal-oriented lifestyles, and yet it opens potentials for deeper wisdom. If you practice meditation without expecting anything, then, as Suzuki said, "Eventually you will resume your own true nature. That is to say, your own true nature resumes itself" (S. Suzuki 1979, 49).

BEYOND DUALITY

Enlightenment is not conceptual. Zen Buddhists explain that as soon as you start to conceptualize, you set up duality. One becomes two: you the thinker and the idea or concept you are thinking about. Then comes further division: I like this; I don't like that. This is right; that is wrong. These dualities are the source of problems and suffering. According to Buddhism, dividing up our world in this way is false. Things do not either exist or not exist, they do both. Everything is just as it is, and the enlightened person perceives things just as they are.

Realizing enlightenment is like waking up from a dream, leaving the shadows of former, limited views behind. Enlightenment welcomes wholeness in the present moment of awareness. "When the ten-thousand things are viewed in their One-ness we return to the Origin and remain where we have always been" (Sheng-Ts'an, in Ross 1960, 271).

Living Zen

When you follow Zen's Path
Through action with heart
Chaotic worlds of discord
Are a symphony of art
—C. Alexander Simpkins

Zen is best learned by doing Zen, by meditating. Meditation can be a quiet, inward experience of sitting with yourself for a certain amount of time each day. It can also be learned in action, by participating meditatively in any activity. Traditionally Zen was taught through a number of arts that came to be known as Zen arts. Part III allows you to engage in ancient traditions, adapted to modern life so that you can easily step right into the spirit of Zen, journeying along the Path in your own unique way.

CHAPTER 9

Meditation Lights the Way

Man must be master of himself, intellectually, morally, and spiritually. To be so,
he must be able to examine his own states of consciousness and direct his
thoughts and desires to the end where lies the rationale of existence.
—Soyen 1987, 146

Meditation is the cornerstone of Zen. Without people actually engaged in meditating, Zen would not be Zen. The Japanese word zen translates as "meditation." All sects of Zen practice meditation, even though they may vary on customs, traditions, and other aspects of Zen life. Meditation is the means to experience Zen for yourself. Dogen believed that zazen was the "right entrance to the Buddha Dharma" (Dogen, in Abe 1992, 17). Since meditative practice itself is enlightenment, there is nothing outside the mind to seek, and nothing outside meditation to do.

Meditation begins in a quiet, seated position. Eventually, you will learn how to sustain your meditative awareness while being active throughout the day.

MEDITATION RESEARCH

A research group in Tokyo performed an interesting set of experiments using experienced Zen monks as subjects. The experimenters measured the brainwave patterns of the monks while they meditated. The researchers found that the EEG undergoes a definite change during Zen meditation that differs distinctively from sleep, deep relaxation, and hypnosis. Monks with eleven to fifteen years' experience had the most striking patterns. Within a very few minutes, the EEG showed a lowering of cerebral activity. There were significant physiological effects as well. The report stated:

> *Zen meditation exercise strengthens the inward concentration, helping to preserve or restore a constant and steady condition of the organism. Zen words "calm, pure-and-serene self" seem to indicate the inward part of the whole organism. (Hirai 1974, 82)*

During one set of tests, meditating monks remained fully aware of clicking sounds made by the experimenters. The monks perceived and registered the sounds accurately without disturbing their meditation. The experimenters concluded that Zen meditation is "relaxed awakening with steady responsiveness" (Hirai 1974, 115).

WHAT IS MEDITATION?

> *Still music*
> *Quiet sound*
> *Deep water*
> *Silent ground*
> —*C. Alexander Simpkins*

Zen meditation draws from ancient Eastern practices of training the mind. In the West, people train their minds through years of schooling, during which they learn how to observe, reason, and learn. Through the methods of observation and conclusion, by inductive and deductive reasoning, Western thinkers come to gain an understanding of their world. Meditative training uses different methods. Zen meditation practitioners turn their attention away from the standpoint of reasoning and learning, and toward what they consider more fundamental ground: intuitive wisdom.

Zen's approach to meditation differs from other forms of meditative practice. For example, adherents of Amida Buddhism repeat a chant—*Namu amida butsu* (the name of Amida the Buddha)—over and over, filling the mind completely, hoping to open the gates of Paradise. Meditations on mantras, the specialty of transcendental meditation, are similar.

Zen takes an opposite yet in some ways complementary approach. Zen meditators let go of focusing on things and self to discover the calm, the silence within. This is not done by turning attention on the outer environment, but rather by sitting quietly with oneself, observing thoughts as they come and letting them go. Here, in complete identity with emptiness, meditation is enlightenment.

MEDITATION PRACTICE

The best way to learn about Zen is to meditate. Understanding Zen must come from experience. The following exercises will give you an opportunity to try Zen meditation. Start with a very short amount of time and increase the duration as you begun to feel able to stay with it.

The type of practice that Zen advocates is beyond technique; it is the way of no technique. Thus, in Zen meditation, the practitioner is never told what to think, but rather to think of nothing, to allow the mind to be empty and free.

Some forms of Zen offer positions for sitting. For example, the instructions for zazen are very specific on how to sit, how to breathe—even what to wear and the type of environment in which to do it. But this instruction is not meant to be anything more than what it is: a clearly defined, suggested way to sit. Ultimately, meditation is one with technique: not just technique, and yet only technique.

WARM-UPS TO ZEN MEDITATION

People new to meditation should begin with a simple exercise to help train attention for Zen meditation. The following exercises will help you prepare.

Breathing

Focusing on breathing is an ancient exercise that draws your attention inward. Since breathing is easily accessible to concentration, it is a good place to begin. Sit on a cushion on the floor with your legs crossed. Let your hands rest comfortably in your lap or draped over your knees. Close your eyes. Turn your attention to your breathing. Notice how the air enters your nose as you inhale lightly. Pay attention to the air as it moves into your nose and goes down into your lungs. Notice how your chest expands and lifts naturally as the air moves down, then drops slightly as the air moves out. Do not try to force or alter your breathing in any way. Merely try to keep your attention on it. Can you notice how your breathing takes care of itself and yet you are completely at one with it? In other words, you do not make yourself breathe, you simply are breathing. Keep bringing your attention back to your breathing if it wanders away. As you become more adept, you will be able to stay with this for longer periods of time.

In this first meditation you can begin to experience Oneness with meditation. Beginners sometimes think they must control their breathing. Try to allow yourself to breathe automatically without interfering, while at the same time maintaining your awareness of your breathing. If you can allow natural, uninhibited breathing with full attention, you will begin to catch a glimpse of the Zen mind.

Zazen—Seated Meditation

The most common practice is seated meditation. Remember, details of technique are not the central issue: the quality of your meditation is. These instructions are guidelines that are commonly followed for zazen. Experiment for yourself.

Sit on a small pillow on the floor with your legs crossed. Some people like to use the full lotus position, feet overlapping the thighs. Others sit in the half lotus, with one foot resting on the opposite thigh, or even in a simple cross-legged position. Keep your back relatively straight, head pointing straight ahead, eyes half-closed. Relax your face, shoulders, and arms. Let your hands rest in your lap, palms up, with one hand resting in the palm of the other, thumbs touching. Allow your breathing to be relaxed and let go of any unnecessary tensions.

Begin by sitting with your mind clear, not thinking about anything in particular. As a thought comes up, become aware of it, but then return to not thinking. Keep returning to not thinking. Your thoughts will slow down and eventually stop as you remain awarely at one with no-thought, empty mind.

Walking Meditation

Some people have difficulty sitting still. Zen practice has taken this into account, integrating a tradition of meditative walking into the daily regime.

As with all Zen meditations, you can do this alone or with a group of meditators.

Find an open space, indoors or out, where you can walk slowly without interruption. Stand straight, with hands lightly clasped in front of you, in the same position as in seated meditation. Take a step forward, heel to toe, slowly. Pay close attention as you notice your foot coming into contact with the floor. Feel your weight shift from the back foot to the front foot. Continue to step slowly, keeping your attention on every aspect of walking. You can step around in a circle or walk where you have a clear path. Breathe comfortably. You may want to exhale as you step down and inhale as you extend the next step. As with meditative breathing, allow yourself to walk naturally and smoothly, just as you do when you are not thinking about it, yet remain aware. This is the paradox of Zen meditation: to be deliberately spontaneous. When you find yourself doing this, you will be experiencing Zen.

Meditation on Work

Work of some kind was always part of the daily routine in Zen monasteries. Monks in rural Korea and Japan often worked side by side with the farmers in the fields. The Chinese Zen monk Pai-chang was the first to officially make work part of Zen. His famous statement "A day without work is a day without food" became the first rule for all Zen monastic life. By including work, Zen does not intend that people stop meditating to go work. Instead, practitioners are expected to carry Zen awareness into their work. As in the other meditative exercises, you learn to allow your work to flow at its best as you stay in tune and aware. The following exercise gives you a brief sample of meditation on work.

Choose a short period of time during your work day to practice meditative work. Decide ahead of time what portion of your work you will do: a page to type, a program to create, a cabinet to nail together, a meeting to attend. Before you begin, sit for a moment or two to gather yourself for meditation. Focus your attention, clear your mind of extraneous thoughts as best you can and bring your attention to this moment. Next, walk over to your work. If you are sitting at a desk, notice what you feel as you sit. If you work with a tool, become very aware of the tool as you hold it or look at it. If you work with computers, let your hands rest gently on the keyboard and pay attention before you begin. Notice all the sensations you have. Begin to do the work. Keep your attention clearly on the task, but try not to interfere. Allow yourself to work efficiently, awarely. If your mind wanders away from the work, bring it back, just as you did in the other meditative exercises. When you are finished, stop, clear your mind, and relax.

As you become accustomed to meditating on your work for short periods of time, experiment with sustaining it longer. The Zen monks strove to approach all aspects of life with meditative awareness.

KOAN PRACTICE

> When the importance of the koan is understood, we may say that more than the half of Zen is understood. The Zen masters, however, may declare that the universe itself is a great living, threatening koan challenging your solution, and that when the key to this great koan is successfully discovered all other koans are minor ones and solve themselves, and, therefore, that the main thing in the study of Zen is to know the universe itself . . . —Suzuki 1994, 11

Suzuki viewed the koan as a means of attaining "one-pointedness of mind"—concentration. From there, the inner search may begin. The koan leads the student away from taken-for-granted thinking, to the horizon of reason, the parameters of what the student can conceive. From there, the committed student steps out to the precipice of the impasse, deep in meditation on the koan. The impasse can only be resolved by a breakthrough into enlightened consciousness through a new, intuitive use of the mind. The instructions that follow have been given to countless students of Zen. Experiment for yourself.

Modern and Traditional Koans

You have now read about Zen masters who let go of all their worldly possessions to devote themselves wholeheartedly to complete emptiness. You have thought about emptiness, perhaps even been baffled by it. Hoping to understand it better, you may have begun to meditate, experimenting with being aware here and there during your day. But, often, the usual thoughts and concerns of everyday life loom large in the foreground of consciousness, and you feel pushed and pulled by the circumstances surrounding you.

Zen koans can bring you to the discovery of the utter freedom of enlightenment. You may find that it happens in a sudden flash or after a long and challenging effort. Both the two koans included here open the possibility. One is a modern adaptation, the other a classic koan. Try both or choose one. There are many ways to work on a koan. Begin by presenting yourself with the question. Keep it in mind as you begin searching. The answer is non rational, calling upon intuitive experiencing. Stay with it as fervently as you would strive to find cool water if marooned on a hot desert island.

Modern Koan

Can you think about nothing without thinking anything about it?

Classic Koan: Chao-chao's "Mu"

Chao-chao's Mu is the first koan given in the *Mumonkan*. It is considered by many Zen masters, past and present, to be a primary entrance into the Way.

A monk asked Chao-chao, "Does a dog have Buddha nature?" Chao-chao answered, "Mu."

In Mumon's comment on this koan, he states that all who wish to learn Zen must pass through the same gates as the Patriarchs. He called his book *Mumonkan* (The Gateless Gate). He believed that "Mu" was the front gate to Zen. If you are able to pass through it, then you will be face-to-face with all who have ever done Zen before you.

Mumon suggests that the only way to accomplish this is to stay with it. He advised: "Employ every ounce of your energy to work on this 'Mu.' If you hold on without interruption, behold: a single spark, and the holy candle is lit!" (Sekida 1977, 28).

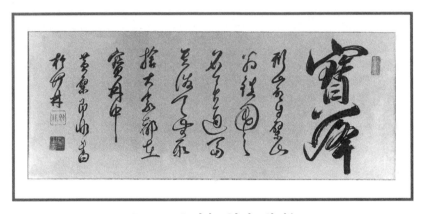

Treasure Peak by Obaku Skuhi

CHAPTER 10

Entering Zen Through the Arts

Art is studied in Japan not only for art's sake, but for spiritual enlightenment.
—D. T. Suzuki in Herrigel, G. 1958, xiii

When Westerners were introduced to Zen, they were often encouraged to use the learning of a Zen art as a doorway into Zen experience. Eugen Herrigel (d. 1955), one of the first Westerners to formally learn Zen in Japan, was told that he would be taught Zen only if he agreed to study a Zen art. He chose archery, and his wife, Gustie, picked flower arranging. We encourage you to experiment with one or several of the Zen arts described in Part III. When you enter into a Zen art, you not only learn artistic skills, but you also develop your mind in the Zen way. This is a viable pathway to experience enlightenment.

Many different kinds of Zen arts are practiced today. Some of the best known are Cha-no-yu (the art of tea), calligraphy, haiku (poetry), and martial arts. There are also the Zen arts of gardening, koto (incense), sumi-e (ink painting), kyudo (archery), Noh drama, and ikebana (flower arranging). Another area that has been influenced by Zen is psychotherapy. Several contemporary Zen masters are also psychotherapists, and some psychotherapists use aspects of Zen in their method or healing rituals.

Some of the arts that are considered as Zen arts may seem to be diametrically opposite, such as martial arts and painting. Despite the outward appearance of difference, at the level of mind, much is the same: the sword and the brush are One. A swordsman learns to use the sword to cut with exact precision. In a life-and-death battle, there are no second chances. This requires an absolutely focused mind, at one with movement. The same presence of mind is necessary for painting. Once the brush is "charged" with paint, there is only one correct stroke. Ink on rice paper will not erase, just as an incorrect cut with the sword cannot be removed. In feudal Japan, many masters of swordfighting were also masters of calligraphy.

What draws all these arts together to make them Zen arts, and what distinguishes a Zen art from other forms of art? As in all other arts, Zen arts offer structure to follow and skills to gain. Yet mastery in a true Zen art cannot be achieved without going through a transformation. The master's instructions bring about a change in the student. The change involves more than simply adding new skills; it also brings about an alteration of consciousness, much like what is achieved through Zen meditation. In fact, Zen arts are a form of meditation, both for the artist and for the audience.

Zen arts epitomize the relationship between form and emptiness. The Heart Sutra tells us that form is emptiness and emptiness is form—a central theme in Zen, as we have discussed in Part II. Walk in a Zen garden and you step into the world of Zen's experience. You feel and see the principles come alive for you in form and space. View a Zen painting and you are offered a profound view of Zen's themes. But what does this really mean?

Zen arts show us. Imagine that you have a blank piece of paper. When you pick it up and look at it, you know what you have—paper without anything written on it. But if a Zen artist paints on that blank sheet of paper a small bird perched on bamboo gazing out over an infinite horizon, everything changes. Now you have form: the bird, the bamboo, the horizon. You also have emptiness, as the bird's gaze draws your eye onto a vast expanse beyond the horizon. It is only out of form that emptiness becomes possible. In Zen, you do not strive to delete all thoughts to make your mind empty. Rather, you discover the emptiness that is already present within the form of thoughts, experiences, and realities.

Each type of Zen art works with form in its own way to bring about the experience of emptiness. In Noh drama, the void is expressed as movement juxtaposed against nonmovement, rhythms to nonrhythms, chorus followed by silence. In painting and calligraphy, empty space is as important as lines. Haiku sparingly uses evocative words, linked to symbolic meanings to express emptiness. For example, in the haiku below, we are offered an image of silence. Formlessness emerges from form.

A heavy snowfall . . .
Disappears into the sea.
What silence!
(Shigematsu 1988, xxv)

Zen arts also differ from other forms of art in that they are goalless. This would seem to be a contradiction, since doing art produces a product, something that comes out of the effort, like a painting, a poem, a performance—a work of art. But for masters of Zen arts, if you try to make a painting or to write a poem, you will inevitably fail. Instead, Zen artists approach their subject without a preconceived thought or plan of what it should be. The artist who did the painting on the cover of this book, Carmen Simpkins, was asked to paint a pelican. This is a common request in Florida, where she lives and paints. Simpkins set herself to begin. Her brush moved in its way as she expressed her artistic nature. The final product was not merely a representation of a pelican. Instead the artist had rendered the deeper spirit of beach, bird, water, and sky. Although it was not what the customer expected, he was overcome by its beauty. Then he truly understood pelican nature. In the process of creating, the artist is lost in the artistic moment. Then the creation springs from its own true nature. The artist does not know what will be created. It simply happens.

Zen artists immerse themselves fully in their art. In the beginning, with deliberate, personal intention, the artist works meditatively, focused on the work, not separate from it. As time passes, a transformation begins to take place. The artist learns to express the art, setting aside concerns of personal ego to allow the medium to speak for itself. Most people have experienced this Oneness in action during brief moments. To be able to call it forth during the act of creation takes time and careful training in both art and meditation. Mature Zen art is selfless and purposeless, flowing out of the unity between the artist and the work, technician and technique, creator and creation.

ZEN ARTS EXERCISES

You learn Zen by participating in and experiencing Zen. In Japan and China, certain arts were developed in the Zen Way, but you can also apply Zen principles to contemporary arts. The choice of content is not the issue; it is the mental and spiritual orientation that is primary.

The following sections instruct you in several accessible traditional Zen arts. We encourage you to experiment for yourself. If you find that you are especially drawn to one, find a good teacher—a master who can guide you to develop and grow as a Zen artist. You may also decide to apply a Zen approach to a contemporary art or activity that you already know—a sport, a craft, an instrument you play, drawing, sculpture etc. You may be surprised at the new possibilities you discover when you take your art along the Zen path of creation.

What Is Your Zen Art?

Is there a Zen art in your life? It can be something active, like playing a sport, or something quiet. Try meditating before, during, and right after a job that you need to do or something you do for recreation. Does your awareness become deeper? Do you find the quality of your attention enhanced at other times of the day? Experiment with many different things, from a very brief task to a larger, more involving activity. Enjoy the Path as you travel along.

CHAPTER 11

Ikebana: Sensitivity to the Flower Nature

The art of flower arrangement is not, in its truest sense, an art, but rather the expression of a much deeper experience of life. The flowers should be arranged in such a way that we are reminded of the lilies of the field, whose beauty was not surpassed by Solomon in all his glory
—D. T. Suzuki, in G. Herrigel 1958, xiv

The Way of flowers is not just a method for arranging flowers but also shapes character and opens the heart to the beauty in life. As flower master Bokuyo Takeda said, "Correct handling of flowers refines the personality" (Herrigel 1958, 35). As with the other Zen arts, in flower arrangement technique is secondary to the inward maturation that takes place. By focusing on something beautiful, such as flowers, you find its beauty reflected within.

Flower arrangement is known as ikebana in Japanese. The word *kebana* means to make cut flowers come alive. The master's sensitive attunement helps bring out the true nature of the flowers for all to see.

Flower arranging was first brought to Japan along with Buddhism as floral offerings to the Buddha. Later, very simple single-flower arrangements became associated with the tea ceremony, called Chabana, or "tea arrangement." Ikebana was a man's art until 1868, when women joined the practice and helped it develop into a highly evolved art form.

Today, a number of ikebana styles sensitively create different effects. *Rikka,* the earliest form of ikebana, has its roots in the Buddhist offerings. Five or more different branches are arranged to emphasize harmony. *Nageire* masters work with three main branches to give the flowers a natural, thrown-in feeling. In *moribana,* arrangements also have three branches, but they are placed in a low wide vase. *Shoka,* "living flower," attempts to show the natural growth cycle of a plant, from its birth as a seed to full maturity. A free-form style developed around 1890 was called *jiyuka.* Although it shares the values of harmony, beauty, and grace with the older forms of ikebana, jiyuka has few restrictions.

Arranging is done in meditative silence to allow maximum sensitivity to the flowers themselves. Flowers are handled tenderly and slowly. The road to mastery in this art is an inner experience, one's own discovery of the flower nature. Traditionally, the flower masters of Japan did not give detailed instructions for their students to follow. The students observed attentively as the master created an arrangement. Then they would work with their own flowers, in synchrony with the master's spirit. Technique was secondary, deriving from the principles and spirit of the style.

One simple principle that is part of many styles of flower arrangement is the Principle of Three. We live in a three-in-one relationship with the spirit of nature, living nature, and ourselves. Yet we often feel alienated from our environment. The flower Way brings us back to our interrelationship with nature, a blending of the personal ego with the flowers. Then, three-in-One can be experienced: spirit of nature, nature, and you.

Flower Arrangement Instructions

Materials

The materials you need for flower arranging are fairly simple. Three separate branches of flowers just as they occur in nature, with leaves intact, are the main materials. Willow branches are commonly used.

A Y-shaped fork, called a *kubari,* is cut from a pliable small branch to be used as a support. The kubari is inserted into the vase about one or two inches down from the top. Prepare this ahead of time so that you are certain that it fits firmly but not too tightly into the container.

The vase should be fairly plain and natural-looking. Traditionally, a bamboo vase was used, but you can use anything that does not overpower the flowers. You will also need a strong pair of pruning shears and a small saw for cutting the branches. A towel will be helpful to wipe up water and leaves. A cup of water will allow you to freshen the flowers once they are arranged.

Preparing Yourself

Before you begin, first quiet your mind. The entire flower arranging process should be performed slowly and calmly, with inner balance. Thus, as you set out your materials, do so with unhurried, poised movements. Then sit quietly in meditation until your mind is clear and you feel centered in the moment.

Working with the Flowers

When you feel ready, examine each branch for elasticity, shape, length, color, aroma, and texture. Notice as much about the flowers as you can. Place the kubari into the vase. Then position the longest flower in the stand. Place the other two so that they seem to be growing from the longer branch. Make any cuts necessary to form your arrangement. The meditative awareness you achieve with your flowers can stay with you the entire day.

ZEN ARTS IN EVERYDAY LIFE: GARDENING

Anything you do—your job, work, family life, hobbies—can be approached in a Zen Way. Life can be lived as an art. Experiment. Can you discover a Zen art in your own everyday life? The following exercise can set you on the Path.

Gardening is an activity many people enjoy. Zen has developed a unique style of gardening that gives the viewer a distinct Zen experience. One type of Zen garden is simple, even stark, with no flowers or color of any kind. The garden is enclosed in a set space and consists only of large stones, small pebbles, and sand raked in a simple pattern. Zen shows that we can perceive emptiness through form. Thus the Zen garden creates empty space between the rocks. Some of the rocks are partially buried in the sand; others sit perched on top of it, spaced asymmetrically. The strong relationship between foreground rocks and background sand shows the interdependence of form and emptiness. The garden remains unmoving but our view of it is always changing. "What we see in the rectangular enclosure, in short, is what we are" (Ross 1960, 111).

Gardening Exercise

This type of Zen garden is very specific in its style. but you can apply Zen to your own gardening. First, gather your tools—clippers, rake, hoe, and so on. Before you begin, meditate until you feel ready. Then set to work: Look carefully at your plants. Feel the texture of the branches, the leaves. Smell the flowers, the soil. Simplify your design, leaving out what is extra. Take into account the interrelationships. Give as much attention to the spaces between plants as you do to the plants themselves. Work quietly, with awareness, and sensitivity. When you are finished, clear away your tools.

CHAPTER 12

Cha-no-yu: The Tea Way to Overcome Stress

*This whole idea of Teaism is a result of this Zen conception of
greatness in the smallest incidents of life*
—Okakura 1989, 71.

Tea ceremonies were linked with Zen from the early years in China, when Zen
patriarchs gathered around a picture of Bodhidharma to share tea together. Tea
drinking when done in the Zen manner, renews the spirit and brings us in close
communion with our inner nature.

The tea ceremony found its greatest development in Japan. One of the
first men to be recognized for achieving Zen enlightenment through tea was
Mokichi Shuko (1453-1502). It was he who introduced the proper setting for
tea ceremonies: away from the busy routines of everyday life. He encouraged
his fellow Japanese to use locally created, handmade pottery rather than

decorative porcelain imported from China. In the spirit of Shuko, we, too, encourage you to use simple pottery, possibly handcrafted by a local artisan.

Sen no Rikyu (1521-1591) developed the ceremony that is practiced today. Deeply imbued with the Zen spirit, the Tea Way, like the Zen Way, should be "nothing special," as he expressed in this poem:

> *Tea is naught but this*
> *First you make the water boil*
> *Then infuse the tea*
> *Then you drink it properly*
> *That is all you need to know. (Sadler 1994, 102).*

This "nothing special" embodies four Zen virtues: harmony, tranquillity, purity, and reverence. These qualities are revealed in the tea ceremony, making it a worthwhile experience.

Harmony, also translated as "gentleness of spirit" (D. T. Suzuki 1973, 274), refers to equanimity with the surroundings. Lighting in the tearoom is subdued, sounds are soft, and all utensils are handled delicately. Tea masters also manifest this gentleness of spirit by being inwardly calm and even-tempered as they quietly prepare the tea.

An atmosphere of gentle harmony pervades the entire tea ceremony. Within this atmosphere, all is tranquil. Tea offers a quiet, calm time away from the fast pace of everyday life. Tranquillity in the environment penetrates inward to the thoughts and emotions of all participants. Inner and outer are unified and calm. The entire ritual is practiced until it can be performed without thought. Then the Buddhist principle of nonduality can be expressed in the tea master's tranquil movements, free of hesitation.

Tea ceremonies remain pure, without adornments or extras. True to Zen emptiness, nothing is added. Only the utensils needed to prepare and serve the tea are used. Without any excess, the tea master can appreciate each object.

This deeply felt warmth for one's possessions, especially when they are well-worn and long-used, is called *sabi*. Sabi deepens over time, like the soft glow of a patina on aged wood. As this experience generalizes to living with fewer material things in all areas of life, a person is said to have *wabi*, which is finding fulfillment in inner richness instead of depending on outer wealth as the source of happiness.

When we experience ourselves as one small part of nature, we feel reverence. Zen teaches that we should feel reverence for all beings no matter how insignificant they might seem. From the enlightened vantage point, we should appreciate everything equally, from the most basic and small to the most complex and vast. Each has the whole reflected within. The tea ceremony represents this relationship. The tearoom, the utensils, the tea, and every action is treated with reverence for its being.

Imperfection may seem like a curious virtue, yet Zen Buddhists believe that perfection is an illusion. The tea Way is to accept, appreciate, and revere what naturally occurs, just as it is. Nature is perfect in its imperfection. Rikyu showed his understanding of this early in his training. He was asked to sweep the walk to the teahouse. When every bit of dust was gone he shook the overhanging limb of a tree until several leaves fell on the path. "Now it is perfect!" he said.

To Rikyu, all the tea values find expression everywhere and in everything:

When you take a sip
From the bowl of powder tea
There within it lies
Clear reflected in its depths
Blue of sky and gray of sea. (Rikyu, in Sadler 1967, 107)

Over the years, some tea ceremonies have come to include a meal. Others are done with dessert, or tea alone. Exact ceremonies were developed as well, with precise instructions for both the tea master, "the host," and the "guests." You can perform a simple tea ceremony when you are in the midst of pressures and deadlines as a way to help you approach your task calmly. With the concerns of the world temporarily at a distance, tea can become a pathway to enlightened experience and later performance.

INSTRUCTIONS FOR A TEA CEREMONY

In the past, Japanese tea ceremonies were performed in a separate teahouse, a small, wooden structure, often likened to Thoreau's cottage on Walden Pond in its rustic simplicity. However, you can experience tea in your own home or garden. Although the outer environment helps to intensify feelings, the spirit of tea ultimately comes from within.

Find a quiet corner of your home and prepare it ahead of time. Clear the space of furniture. Place a simple mat on the floor and bring in a small plant, a simple flower arrangement, or a single picture. You can burn soothing incense, but not anything too heavy. Japanese tea masters often used incense from tropical trees that had been buried underwater for many years (D. T. Suzuki 1973, 299). Decorations should be arranged according to each occasion and the particular guests. Keep it very simple and unadorned. If you do not have an indoor space, look for a quiet place outside.

Gather your utensils: teapot, teacups, water, and tea. You will also need a heat source, such as a small hibachi, hot plate, or hot coals in a fireplace. You can choose from several types of tea. The traditional way is to use powdered tea and a whisk to stir it. Most tea today comes as leaves, prepared by steeping. Use whatever you can find: The spirit of tea transcends any particular technique or method. Practice preparing tea until you can do it smoothly with your mind clear and focused.

When you are ready, bring in your guests. In Japanese teahouses, the entry door is low so that people have to crouch down to enter. Traditionally, emperors and peasants alike entered with head bowed. Everyone is equal in the tearoom. Try to foster the atmosphere of mutual respect at your own tea ceremony. Do not engage in talking, except for simple greetings and instructions. Invite your guests to sit on the floor, facing each other. Encourage them to pay close attention as you prepare the tea. Tell them to meditate on what they see, hear, smell, feel, and taste.

Enjoy the tranquillity, free for a short time of obligations. Following tea, mind cleared and awareness sharpened, you may discover renewed energy with which to face your responsibilities.

CHAPTER 13

Poetic Voice, Enlightened Expression

Sand, breeze, sun
Join with primeval sea
Synthesize as One
Experience unity
—C. Alexander Simpkins

Poetry has been used by Zen monks since the beginnings of Zen and has continued to play a pivotal role in Zen's evolution. Poems are often metaphorical, allowing Zen practitioners to point the way with words. Ideas that are difficult to communicate often become clearer through poetry.

From the very beginning, poetry was the preferred way to express Zen. Bodhidharma's famous description of Zen as a special transmission outside of words and letters was written as a poem (see the opening of Chapter 5). The first recorded explanation of Zen, the "Hsin Hsin Ming" composed by the Third Chinese Patriarch, Seng-ts'an, reveals Zen's approach of nonduality in poetry. Here is the last stanza:

> *One thing is all things*
> *All things are one thing . . .*
> *What is dual is not the believing mind*
> *Beyond all language,*
> *For it there is no past, no present, no future. (Blyth 1964, 102)*

The importance of poetry in Zen's history continued with Hui-neng, the Sixth Patriarch. As we described in Chapter 2, Hui-neng's poem greatly impressed Hung-jen, convincing him that this wise lay monk should start his own school of Zen. Because of a poem, Hui-neng's Sudden Enlightenment branch of Zen was sanctioned.

Following Hui-neng, many Zen practitioners used poetry to express enlightenment. Muso (1275-1351), the national teacher of Japan, had been traveling from monastery to monastery, searching unsuccessfully for enlightenment. One evening, feeling exhausted and frustrated, Muso leaned back against what he thought was a garden wall. But the wall was not where he expected it to be, and he fell over. In that moment, he found enlightenment! Here is his enlightenment poem:

> *For many years I dug the earth and searched for the blue heaven,*
> *And how often, how often did my heart grow heavier and heavier.*
> *One night, in the dark, I took stone and brick,*
> *And mindlessly struck the bones of the empty heaven. (Dumoulin 1990, 157)*

Hakuin, one of Japan's most influential monks, composed many works of art during his long career. His poem "Zazenwasan" has helped many students to discover their buddha mind. The final lines read:

At this very moment, what is there more for you to seek,
With nirvana itself manifest before you?
This very place, this is the Lotus Land;
This very body, this is Buddha. (Dumoulin 1990, 394)

POETRY EXERCISE

After you have meditated, or perhaps following a meaningful experience, experiment with writing your own enlightenment poem. Express yourself directly, without interpretation or judgment.

HAIKU

[Haiku is] a record of a moment of emotion in which human nature
is somehow linked to all nature.
—*Henderson 1977, 22*

Haiku is a type of poetry that has become associated with Zen. Haiku has a simple but very distinctive format: three lines, seventeen syllables. Much like tea, haiku expresses Zen values. With simplicity to the point of scarcity, this skeletal number of words points to an entire experience. Haiku is not romantic and lacks elaborate sentiments. Like Zen enlightenment, haiku is immediate, expressing the writer's direct experience and bringing the listener with him into the moment. Often the themes center around nature, usually a small occurrence, thereby showing the significance of every moment, like this poem:

A little frog
Riding on a banana leaf,
Trembling.(Kikaku [1660-1707] in D. T. Suzuki 1973, 231)

Basho, (1643-1694) the founder of modern haiku, was one of the most famous Zen haiku poets. His poems cut through to the very essence of the moment. In response to the question, "How are you doing?," posed by his Zen teacher Buccho to test Basho's progress in Zen, Basho is said to have created this haiku: "The moss has grown greener since the rain."

Buccho, wanting to know if Basho's understanding went deeper, asked, "What Zen is there before the moss was greener?"

Basho answered with enlightened spirit:

The old pond, ah!
A frog jumps in:
The water's sound.

The image of the frog's splash is one of the most famous Zen haiku. Basho's haiku communicates his direct experience at that particular moment.

Haiku is the revealing of this preaching [Dharma] by presenting us with the thing devoid of all our mental twisting and emotional discoloration; or rather it shows the thing as it exists at one and the same time outside and inside the mind, perfectly subjective; ourselves undivided from the object in its original unity with ourselves. (Blyth 1969, 270)

Instructions for writing Haiku

You can write your own haiku. The rules for classical Japanese haiku are fairly simple. Each poem has seventeen syllables and three lines, with the form of five-seven-five. There should be some reference to nature as it occurs now as a particular, concrete event or experience. Generalizations and abstractions are not considered Zen haiku.

English haiku may deviate somewhat from the exact syllable count, although three lines is fairly universal. The idea is to keep the poem short, to express yourself with a minimum of words. Keep the rules in mind as guidelines to help you get in touch with your poetic Zen spirit.

Jittoku

CHAPTER 14

Sumi-e: The Stroke of Awareness

Zen painting is the end-product of satori: the way in which it expresses itself pictorially.
—Herrigel, 1971, 52

MANY FORMS: ONE WAY

A Zen master once said, "If you want to see, see right at once" (D. T. Suzuki 1973, 130). Zen ink painting, or sumi-e, is like that—a direct reflection of the Way. Zen paintings have taken on many different forms over the centuries: portrait paintings of patriarchs and buddhas, enlightenment paintings, depiction of events, calligraphy, and landscapes.

Zen paintings differ from traditional Buddhist paintings. Buddha was historically represented in rich colors with fine and decorative detail. These works portrayed Buddha in all his majesty as a heavenly figure, seated in

Ox

deep meditation. Zen practice has always been "nothing special." Ideals and heavenly standards are secondary to inner vision. Zen paintings portray people, even the Buddha himself, as ordinary, human individuals.

Zen paintings show Buddha and the patriarchs engaged in action, as is the Zen Way. Buddha is portrayed holding up a flower, marking the first Zen transmission to Mahakasyapa. In another painting Buddha returns from the mountain following his enlightenment. Numerous paintings tell the many stories of Bodhidharma: for example, facing the cave wall in meditation.

Some Zen paintings capture the moment of an individual's enlightenment. True to the Zen spirit, the subject of these pictures can be very ordinary, just as enlightenment often occurs in the midst of everyday life. Sometimes Zen paintings portrayed an early Chinese patriarch's enlightenment along-side his enlightenment poem. Others showed enlightened individuals. One famous example is Pu-tai (Ho-tei), a jolly fellow, sometimes called the Chinese Santa Claus, who carried a large sack and always had a kindly twinkle in his eye.

The Oxherd pictures, a series of eight to ten drawings depicting the journey to enlightenment, have been recreated by many different artists. The story unfolds in each picture, drawn inside a circle. First the oxherd searches for the ox. Then he is shown noticing its footsteps, perceiving the ox, catching it, taming it, and riding it home. Next the oxherd transcends the ox and is pictured meditating. In the eighth picture, an empty circle, both ox and self are transcended. Later versions add two more pictures: finding enlightenment, then returning to the world as an enlightened Bodhisattva to help others. The oxherd says, "I visit the wineshop and the market, and everyone I look upon becomes enlightened" (Reps 1994, 186).

Zen has always been a close friend of nature. Since everything has Buddha-nature, "Rivers and streams, the earth are all manifestations of the divine body of the Law" (Awalawa 1981, 28). Artists represent their oneness with nature through expressive strokes of the brush that suggest form in flux, as is the passage of time. You can almost see the leaves rustle in the breeze.

THE MEDIUM IS THE MESSAGE

> *Long, short, far, or near*
> *What is need not be an object of thought*
> *Lest we obscure our vision*
> *That is already clear.*
> —*C. Alexander Simpkins*

Zen paintings are usually done in black ink, using simple brush strokes to communicate Zen. The words of Marshall McLuhan are most apt: "The medium is the message." Zen painters did not develop original techniques that were uniquely their own, yet the style in which ink is applied gives these paintings distinction. Fluid mediums, gradual washes, and splashed ink are some of the techniques used. The result is an abstract style, sometimes more avant-garde than the moderns!

> *The "sketchiness" of a Zen picture is therefore something quite different from what we in the West understand by "sketch." It is an abbreviated statement which concentrates on the essential inner nature of things. (Brinker 1987, 154)*

The simplicity and asymmetry of Zen paintings suggest a deeper look at the scene. The painting takes form as much in the mind of the viewer as on the paper. A simple brush stroke might be a horizon overlooking an infinite vista of emptiness. Form and formlessness interrelate with balance between the white space and the black ink.

Not all sumi-e painting is Zen painting. For example, some sumi-e was influenced by Taoism. In these paintings, a small person is pictured amid a vast vista of mountains and trees to show Oneness with nature. By contrast, Zen sumi-e is simpler, with fewer strokes, often suggesting the picture without clearly showing it.

Japanese Zen exerted a very strong influence on the development and refinement of sumi-e. Zen sumi-e painters freed themselves from rules and techniques in order to express their inner spirit. They painted with sincerity and simplicity, creating works that were quite different from intellectual, representational forms of sumi-e.

ZEN INSPIRES MODERN WESTERN ARTISTS

The influence of Zen filtered into Western contemporary art. Many of the ancient Zen works, created during the early years of Zen, have a decidedly modern look. Thus, Zen continues to appeal to art today. The modern art movement in Europe was greatly influenced by Eastern art and Zen philosophy. Vincent van Gogh (1853-1890) had an interest in Japanese art and was affected by Japanese woodcuts. Wassily Kandinsky (1866-1944), well known for his abstract splashes of color and lines, was aware of the spiritual depth expressed in Zen art. He wrote:

> It is precisely this general "inner tone" that is lacking in the West. Indeed, it cannot be helped: we have turned away, for reasons obscure to us, from the internal to the external. And yet, perhaps we Westerners shall not, after all, have to wait too long before that same inner sound, so strangely silenced, reawakens within us and, sounding forth our innermost depths, involuntarily reveals its affinity with the East—just as in the very heart of all peoples—in the now darkest depths of the spirit, there shall resound one universal sound, albeit at present inaudible to us—the sound of the spirit of man. (Westgeest 1996, 105)

D. T. Suzuki either directly taught or indirectly influenced a number of American artists. John Cage (1912-1992), who studied with Suzuki at Columbia University, applied Zen principles to music in order to become free and spontaneous. He felt that the purpose of Zen was to wake people up, and formulated that his own art was "waking up to the very life we're living" (Cage 1961, 57). He was one of the first musicians to make his audience part of his performance, encorporating the spontaneous sounds they made during the concert into the work itself as it was happening. Always actively engaged in his ideas, Cage gathered many well-known artists and musicians of the day into a creative group, the Club, where they discussed Zen, the *I-Ching,* and existentialism. Abstract artists Franz Kline (1910-1962), Ad Reinhardt (1913-1967), and Rollin Crampton (1886-1976), all members of the Club, were profoundly affected by Zen through Cage, using Zen philosophy to enhance their creativity and spontaneity.

INSTRUCTIONS FOR ZEN SUMI-E PAINTING

The artist strives toward a skilled carelessness in the control of the brush as the coordination between mind, eye, hand, and brush must be such as to give the resulting stroke living spontaneity, strength, and beauty.
—*Ukai Uchiyama, in Thompson 1968, 12*

Sumi-e lends itself well to Zen, since it uses simple materials, few strokes, and uncomplicated themes. Techniques are secondary to spiritual expression in the Zen arts. With this in mind, we encourage you to experiment with these instructions as a means to express your own inner light. Be patient. Devote yourself fully to the art whenever you pick up the brush. This may be brief sessions or a more extended study. The amount of time is not the issue; seek intensity in the moment.

MATERIALS

The tools needed for sumi-e painting are fairly simple: brushes, inkstone, ink, water dishes, and paper. The inkstone, called a *suzuri* is used to mix and hold the ink. Inkstones are usually rectangular in shape, but they may also be round, oval, or naturally shaped. The stone should be smooth and hard. Sumi-e is the name given to the black ink used in sumi-e painting. Traditionally, it came in an ink stick that was mixed with water, but you can also get it in liquid form. There are many different grades of sumi-e with varying opinions on which is best. Ask at your art store for the best brand available.

Use soft, absorbent rice paper, which is actually made of various vegetable fibers. It often comes in large sheets, twenty-seven inches by fifty-four inches, or in rolls. You can practice on newsprint, but using rice paper helps to get the proper "feel" of how the ink is absorbed by the paper.

Sumi-e brushes are made with long bamboo handles. The brushes come in different sizes and types of bristles so you can make different types of strokes. You can start with two or three basic brushes. The outline brush, *menso,* is used for painting thin lines. For softer lines, use a *sokumyo* brush, which is fine like a menso brush but softer. *Mokkutsu* brushes are larger and wider than the outline brushes. They are used for boneless, wash strokes. Shallow dishes, usually white, around six inches or less in diameter, are used to test the blackness of ink and for controlling the amount of the ink on the brush.

Japanese artists spread a large feltlike cloth on the floor and kneel on a small pillow, leaning over their work. If you are not comfortable kneeling on the floor, place your work on a padded (for absorption) table. Sit on a tall stool or chair, or stand so that you can be above your work; just make sure you allow for freedom of arm movement.

Preparation

Before you begin, close your eyes and meditate. Once you feel yourself fully present in the moment and clear of distracting thoughts, ready your tools meditatively. Gather your brushes. Prepare your paper. Bring out your ink, inkholder, dishes. Throughout the process bring your full attention to every aspect of the process. Notice the feel of the brushes. Pay attention to the texture and consistency of the paper. Set everything out carefully. Then sit for a moment and once again clear your mind of all distractions. Breathe in and out, let your arms relax, allow them to move a little, rising and falling with each breath. When you feel ready, begin to work.

Preparing the Ink

Once you have set your tools out, you can ready the ink. Ink and water mixed together will create all the tones you need for sumi-e painting. Thus, the very nature of Zen painting begins with the simplicity of the materials themselves. Fill your water dish with a small amount of water.

If you choose to use an ink stick, you will prepare your ink before each painting session. Approach this task meditatively. Notice how the inkstand slants down into the small well at the end. Pour a small amount of water into the well. Hold the sumi-e stick perpendicular to the stone and rub it back and forth over the surface of the stone, occasionally dipping it into the water. This blending should not be rushed. Use this time to clear your mind as you focus fully on the quiet movements, back and forth. Continue until the sumi-e has the consistency of rich cream with a slightly dull look to the ink. This thick mixture is called *noboku,* thick ink. You can make up two more mixtures of ink to help facilitate your painting. Separate some of the ink into a second shallow dish and add water to create *choboku,* middle ink. Finally, make an even lighter ink, *tomboku,* thin ink that is mostly water.

Holding the Brush

Hold the brush from the upper half, between your thumb and index finger, with the other fingers adding support. Keep your hand relaxed. Experiment for a grip that is comfortable.

Brush Strokes

The brush stroke is the cornerstone of ink painting. These techniques are guidelines. Ultimately, as you begin to get a feel for your work, you will discover your own techniques. Sumi-e painting comes from your felt experience.

Lines are painted freely and confidently, with little hesitation. The best way to learn this is to experiment with some practice strokes. Dip the brush in the water. Then gently squeeze it dry with your fingers, pulling the bristles back into their point. Now dip the brush into one of your ink mixtures, perpendicular to the paper. Keep your wrist straight and move the brush along the paper by making a full arm stroke that comes from your shoulder. Sensitivity for the stroke comes from your fingertips, but the motion flows from your whole arm. Paint swiftly and steadily, keeping the pressure equal throughout the stroke. Experiment with various directions on the paper.

Next try a circle. Use the same stroke but allow your hand, arm, and shoulder to move in one continuous motion. If you practice martial arts you will recognize a similar unity of motion. Once you have a feeling for this free-flowing movement, try other lines and shapes. You can vary the pressure and direction on the paper to get unlimited possibilities. Be bold or gentle, strong or weak—let your expression be free!

Another technique that is unique to sumi-e is the boneless technique (mokkotsu), which is a stroke without any outline. These strokes are usually multitoned and are used in combination with lines. First moisten your brush with water. Then charge it with ink so that the darkest ink is at the tip and

Brushstrokes

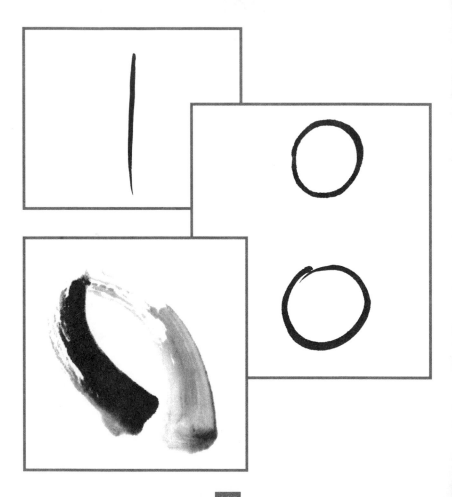

lighter ink moves up the side of the brush. As you stroke the paper with your brush held at an angle, you will get variations of tones. Continue the stroke for as long as you can.

Part of the art of Zen sumi-e is freedom of expression. The old masters created with such originality that the inner spirit was able to shine through. *Iren,* the continuous stroke, is the flowing movement of the sumi-e brush. Just as in calligraphy, and even in regular handwriting, one letter flows into the next. So in sumi-e, continuous strokes flow freely, one to the next. To experiment with this, allow your arm to swing in a series of circular motions. Let the brush touch the paper as you move and begin to create various patterns. You might think of branches or long grass swaying in the wind.

The art of sumi-e is a Oneness between brush, ink, paper, and artist. In time, you begin to gain an inner feel for just the right amount of ink and water, the exact pressure on the paper, and the movement of your brush, at One with the spirit your painting expresses.

CHAPTER 15

Martial Arts: Finding Inner Power

Everything done in karate—every movement, every feeling—can be traced to some principle of Zen. A student overlooking this fact misses the lifeblood of karate.
—Mattson 1963, 30-31

ZEN AND SWORDSMANSHIP

From its early formal beginnings in Japan, Zen was put to practical use. Eisai, credited as the founder of Zen in Japan, trained samurai of the Hojo (1203-1301) shoguns at his monasteries. Zen koans were used to train and develop the attitudes and spirit of samurai, helping them carry out their role as warriors. As the years passed, a training program for samurai including Zen koans became standard curriculum in many Rinzai temples. Samurai students were asked koan questions, as part of their testing. Correct answers were required for certification. The shoguns believed that koan training gave their swordsmen an edge. An accomplished teacher of swordsmanship who saw his pupil master the utmost of his art told him, "Beyond this my instruction must give way to Zen teaching" (Nitobe 1969, 11). This tradition has continued to the present day in some martial arts schools, such as tae chun do, where belt rank exams do not simply require physical skills but also test for deeper understanding through koans.

A story of Hakuin's teacher Shoju Ronin (1642-1721) illustrated this point clearly in a confrontation with an overconfident swordfighter who had been studying with him. The swordfighter made a challenging remark concerning the application of Shoju's Zen: "You may be a great master of Zen and its theory, but in actual combat with a sword, you would be unable to beat me!"

Shoju smiled calmly and answered, "Really, you think so? Well, why don't we test this? Attack me with all your force right now!"

The swordfighter was surprised by Shoju's request and quickly answered, "I couldn't possibly do that! I would kill you."

But Shoju reassured the samurai, "Oh, don't worry. I'll use my fan to show you how it would go."

Now the samurai was intrigued, and so he took a fighting stance, drew his sword, and attacked. But wherever he struck, Shoju evaded, with the fan covering any apparent opening. The Zen master's movements were subtle, quick, and accurate. After several missed swings from the samurai, Shoju stepped closer and touched the samurai's heart with his fan, showing how easily he could have dealt him a killing blow. The samurai felt awe. He bowed and said, "Truly, you are a great martial artist!"

Shoju replied modestly, "The principle is the same, no matter what the application."

Takuan was a renowned Buddhist priest who wrote highly authoritative treatises on Zen for swordsmanship that clearly expressed Zen's tenets. Takuan advised samurai to help them improve their swordfighting through application of Zen no-mind. He taught that when there is nothing in the mind, you are like a wheel turning freely. From the empty center, the sword-fighter functions at his best. If you think about something, thinking stops there. The essence of martial arts, he wrote in a letter to his friend and student swordsman Munenori Yagyu ("The Mysterious Record of Immovable Wisdom" in Takuan, 1986), is that mind should not be detained by anything nor stopped anywhere. Mind must remain empty, allowing attention to flow naturally wherever it needs to go. Then many things are possible, and whatever you have trained yourself to do will be performed automatically, like a flash of lightning.

The ultimate focus is no-focus, beyond distinguishing between self and other. The sword becomes an extension of the swordfighter, and correct technique happens instinctively, in a natural response to the situation. This is made possible by responding to each moment of challenge as it comes, without thought. The ultimate strategy is no-strategy.

As a result of the influence of Takuan and other Zen masters, the tenets of several schools of swordsmanship were profoundly influenced by Zen. Miyamoto Musashi (1584–1645), an incomparable swordsman of feudal Japan, was also a student of Takuan. Musashi wrote the classic guide to strategy, *The Book of Five Rings,* in which he spelled out specific strategies. However, the ultimate in swordfighting techniques was the way of no-technique. He devoted his final chapter to the Void. "Wisdom has existence, principle has existence, the Way has existence, spirit is nothingness" (Musashi 1974, 95).

MARTIAL ARTS

Zen's practical wisdom found its way into many martial arts, and now has a long, honorable history of interaction with a wide variety of styles of contemporary karate, tae kwon do, and kung fu arts. Zen principles and techniques apply to martial arts in many ways, partly in terms of the mental set and martial attitude of practitioners, and partly as a creative stimulus, an analogy for technique and strategy. Takuan believed that technique and spirit were like two wheels of a cart. Perhaps now we would think about them as two wheels of a bicycle. If one wheel is broken, no movement is possible.

Some twentieth century martial arts, such as Duk Sung Son's tae kwon do, embody Zen in action itself. Without using words, Zen is lived by Duk Sung Son's disciplined, down-to-earth, everyday practice of the art. Like Dogen, who encouraged his disciples to meditate with absolute devotion no matter what they might be feeling that day, Duk Sung Son urges his tae kwon do students to exert themselves wholeheartedly in every workout. "Always best!" he yells with conviction.

Tae chun do directly incorporates periods of Zen meditation into workouts and practice. Not only do students sit in meditation, but they also meditate as they perform the physical skills. Unity of mind, body, and spirit generalizes into everyday life.

COURAGE

Martial artists participate in activities such as sparring and self-defense practice that can bring up fears. Yet through training, martial artists learn to face potentially dangerous situations with great courage. How do they manage this? Zen offers a new perspective.

Shoju Ronin believed that a skilled master of Zen should be able to meditate even in the face of danger, and he used his own experience to demonstrate the power of meditation to his students. Once, his village was being terrorized by a hungry pack of wolves. For seven nights, Shoju went out alone into the graveyard and meditated. The wolves approached him, sniffing at his neck and ears. Shoju continued to meditate deeply. The wolves watched and circled, but they left him alone. Shoju believed that the real opponent is not out in the environment but lies within. As he said, "Deluded thoughts are indeed more terrifying than tigers and wolves" (Yampolsky 1971, 74).

Western philosophy holds that courage is a virtue, something to strive for, to have, and to be. There is no question that fear and the anxiety it brings can be extremely troubling. But Zen offers an alternative: to transcend the effort of trying to have courage or be courageous. We cannot escape fear. We can only rise above fear's grip by realizing and accepting its true nature. In Zen, courage and fear do not exist as objects apart from or outside of oneself.

According to Zen, the problem of fear is not in the situation itself, but in our reaction or response to the situation, in our manner of construing reality. Zen invites us to experience something different, something that radically changes the experience of fear. Fear can be overcome by transforming it. The solution is not to suppress fear. Instead, one must change the state into process.

An emotion like fear can be experienced as a transitory emotion like all others when perceived in a different context against the background of Oneness. This new context can change fear's meaning to us. Fear may continue to be felt, but now from a different perspective, integrated within the unity. Though fear and anxiety may still be felt, they are now part of the accepted feeling tone at the time. Fear just is, and also is not. There is only the mysterious moment, with emotional tone, always in process.

Ernest Hemingway said, "Courage is grace under pressure." But in the profound sense, for the Zen Buddhist, every moment is significant. There is no moment with pressure, and yet no moment without pressure. It all matters, and yet nothing matters. These paradoxes are resolved in meditation, as emptiness becomes reality.

DISCIPLINE
Discipline can be difficult to develop, and yet martial artists are known

for their ability to be disciplined. Zen helps the martial artist in training spirit, courage, and discipline. Whether sparring or in everyday conduct, "The effort not to stop the mind in just one place—this is discipline" (Takuan 1986, 32). Zen meditation can help you to develop your own self-discipline, so it can be called forth when needed. Paradoxically, focusing the mind on flowing freely requires great control and discipline: to deliberately be spontaneous! Self-discipline becomes spontaneous and effortless when attention is free from mistaken restriction.

EMPTY MIND EXERCISE

When you interpret a situation with a narrow concept, your mind may become tied down, restricted to related ideas. Then, creative response to the situation at hand is inhibited. Disciplined response cannot spontaneously occur. By contrast, when you free your attention from restraint, you can spontaneously follow every situation directly, just as it is, without preconceptions or post conceptions— without anticipation or afterthought.

Following the instructions for zazen (given in Chapter 9), sit comfortably in a quiet place and meditate. Once you feel relatively clear of thought, look around at your surroundings. If indoors, notice the walls, the furniture with its colors, patterns, spacing—whatever draws your interest. Do not pause or stop to think about what you observe. Let your attention continue to shift freely around the entire room. Allow any associated thoughts and feelings to be, and go with the flow of awareness. Sustain this for a period of time. Then, close your eyes and wait until your thoughts and feelings are quiet and you are done.

Advanced meditators, after practicing regularly, can try this in motion— for example, while taking a walk, sailing or rowing, while riding in a bus or train.

ONENESS OF THOUGHT AND ACTION

In martial arts, one of the most crucial concerns is how to reduce the gap between attack and defense, stimulus and response. If the opponent throws a kick or punch, the defender must react quickly or be hit. An "opening" is that moment, that gap, which corresponds to a hesitation between thought and action. Zen aims directly at this point. Immediate perception, without rational interpretation to slow down reactions, is quicker. If an opponent throws a punch, the martial artist must simply react. Any interpretation, any thought about it, slows the reaction. Respond to the situation as it is, exactly and correctly. No concepts are necessary outside of this. If you accept what is taking place, you can relate to it, as it is.

As Bruce Lee said, "There is no thought, only thusness [suchness]—what is. Thusness does not move, but its motion and function are inexhaustible" (Lee 1979, 21).

Concepts and names bring about reactions as we think about the idea. Then the object being considered is no longer perceived directly, but filtered through our concepts, which slows us down. Zen Buddhists believe that names and concepts can prevent us from experiencing things directly in their suchness. These names and concepts obstruct clear insight, leading to hesitation and conflict. Thought does not lead directly to action if we think about our thought.

> *The owner of the right eye sees each object in its own light. When he sees the sword, he knows at once the way it operates. He confronts the multiplicity of things and is not confounded. (D. T. Suzuki 1973, 204-205)*

In traditional martial arts, this leads to further implications. A fierce, angry, aggressive attitude does not help: It results in poor performance and reactions. Similarly, a timid, fearful, anxious attitude also hinders. All attitudes are transitory illusions. Only the here and now, moment to moment exists. Tension between now and what is to come dissolves into nothingness for the Zen martial artist. Each punch, block, or kick is unique and new, yet not separate or different from others before.

MEDITATION EXERCISE

Meditation can be done while you perform some aspect of your martial art—for example, while sparring. Meditate before you begin, clear your awareness of distractions, focus your attention on each moment. Begin without anything in mind. Simply react and allow your training to express itself. Do not let yourself become annoyed by the other's attacks, nor feel happy or proud if you score a point. Simply react, mind free and unfettered. If you have trained well, you will find that without mental hindrances, you are free to perform at your best.

You can apply this same awareness to other aspects of your martial arts training, such as practising forms, or to sports. Practice without evaluation of your performance. Be directly and fully immersed in the moment-to-moment action.

TRANSCEND TECHNIQUE

Zen training is beyond technique, the Way of No Technique. In Zen meditation, the practitioner is never told what to think; instead, the teacher encourages the student to think of nothing, to allow the mind to be empty and free. Awareness of motion is important in martial arts meditation. Concentration on movement points us away from the periphery of concerns to the center. Zen spirit can be felt and expressed in motion as it is in stillness, coordinating hand and foot as in coordinating mind and body. Form does not differ from emptiness. Form, through martial art, can be used to get in touch with emptiness, the path to enlightenment.

CHAPTER 16

Psychotherapy: Beyond the Void

Steve: What do you experience now?
Pt: I feel...peaceful. Quiet. Calm. Relaxed. I just want to sit here and enjoy it.
Pt: (After several minutes) I'm beginning to feel some trembling in my body.
I want to open my eyes. (looks around the room) Oh! Things look so bright,
so clear. The colors. So vivid! (looks at me) I see you. I think I've never
really seen you before. You know what I mean? (Patient moves around the
room, looking at other members of the group. Everyone is transfixed.)
For a moment, we are all alive—really alive—and we know, all of us, what
it means to be alive and joyful and whole and a part of the universe.
—J. O. Stevens 1975, 147

Zen lends itself to psychotherapy in many ways. It can guide you directly on
a path of self-discovery, or indirectly, along with the insights and methods of

psychotherapy, by pointing to your intuitive being, the source of deeper understanding. We reach back to positive unconscious potential within, before limiting concepts. False self-concepts drop away as we find ourselves genuinely being ourselves.

MENTAL FLEXIBILITY

Over time, we accumulate a set of concepts, beliefs, and assumptions that help us make sense of everyday life. Some arise out of individual life experiences. Others come from family, school, work, and the shared concepts, beliefs, and assumptions held by our culture. These tend to be taken for granted. Our experience of the actual world interacts with our assumptions and concepts about it (Frank, 1991).

Our assumptions may become so habitual, so taken for granted, that unfortunately, sometimes, false limitations seem absolutely real. We may feel trapped, stuck, unable to do our best. But the situational restraints could be illusions from narrow, limiting, or inaccurate concepts that have become habitual. If a new situation or person is presented, we may misrepresent it, and consequently not recognize the positive potential already there in a person or in our situation. Our reactions may be inappropriate and rigid. We may need to change.

> The measure of mental health is flexibility . . . The essence of illness is the freezing of behavior into unalterable and insatiable patterns.
> —Kubie 1975, 20-21

Healthy people learn through experience. They respond appropriately to changing internal and external conditions and alter concepts and behavior when needed. An important part of good therapy is helping patients develop mental flexibility.

Zen teaches that our actions and reactions are just that, no more. Preconceptions and assumptions need not be the center, nor the ultimate parameters, of a situation. We can become more flexible by suspending assumptions. Regular meditation will bring moments of awareness without limitations: perception without conception. Experiment with the following exercise.

Meditative Awareness

Find a place outdoors where you can be undisturbed, perhaps in your backyard or at a park. Sit comfortably and close your eyes. Pay attention to yourself as you sit. Can you feel the ground? Do you notice the air on your skin? Does the sunlight feel warm? Is there a cool breeze? Notice all the details, keep your attention on each moment. Next, extend your attention to your surroundings. Do you hear birds chirping? Can you smell the aroma of grass or trees? Continue to meditate on your experience for several minutes. Each time you do this exercise, try increasing the duration. Experiment with sitting in different environments—such as a quiet room in your house. Always maintain your moment-to-moment awareness without thinking anything about it.

SELF-CONCEPT AND THE TRUE SELF

Western psychotherapy depends on enhancing and clarifying the patient's concept of self. Zen Buddhism, as we have described it in Part II, denies the ultimate reality of the individual self. How can we resolve this contradiction? Is there a way to synthesize these two traditions?

We can find some resolution by considering the self from two complementary levels of perspective: the relative and the absolute. On the relative level, we are all individuals. Each of us is unique, no two are exactly alike. Even identical twins have differences. Every person has an individual self. On the absolute level, however we are part of the unknowable Oneness. Our self nature is a reflection of the greater unity, never separate from our interaction. At this absolute level, no actual objective individual exists. Therefore, we have a self, yet we do not. Relative and absolute levels of relationship complement each other. Each depends on the other. Both are needed and neither is sufficient without the other.

Zen teaches that we should not be caught up in false concerns, including narrow self-concerns, which are only on the relative level. If the concept of self is ultimately an illusion, then it does not make sense to be so concerned with it. Sometimes we spend too much time trying to sort ourselves out. Too much self-analysis can lead us away from ourselves. The true self is the source of change.

Humanistic psychotherapy considers self-actualization the fundamental motivation, the root of behavior. This means that as you become your true self instead of trying to be some image of an ideal self, you will naturally fulfill your potential. As Lin-chi said,

> Blind men! You're putting a head on top of the one you already have. What do you yourself lack! Followers of the Way, your own present activities do not differ from those of the patriarch-buddhas. You just don't believe this and keep on seeking outside. Make no mistake! Outside there is no dharma; inside, there is none to be obtained. (Sasaki 1975, 25)

Exercise in Selflessness

You can experience the no-self of Zen by doing something for others without seeking any reward or recognition. Suzuki called this secret virtue. Volunteer your time and skills for something you care about. Community service organizations, charitable foundations, or seasonal rituals all offer opportunities to practice this. You may decide to do something independently in your neighborhood or on your street. Do not try to get anything in return. Do it in a manageable, time-limited way, for the experience.

Anonymous good deeds help to correct imbalances. Instead of skeletons in the closet, you can have something to secretly feel positive about.

WHOLEHEARTED ACCEPTANCE

Karen Horney was a renowned psychotherapist who was influenced by Zen late in life. She was initially affected by D. T. Suzuki, and then began further study of Zen, as she discovered useful links to therapy. She believed that healthy psychological functioning includes having ideals for yourself. Ideals give people something better to strive for. But the ideal self should never be mistaken for the actual or true self. We are who we are now, striving to be more and better. If we lose this perspective, problems may develop. Psychotherapy helps people discover and become their true selves. When people actualize their true selves, they become wholeheartedly involved in living fully and well. Mental health and a fulfilling life can come from whole-heartedness— living and acting in harmony with our real self. Zen guided Horney's insights about the nature of the true self:

> It is actually accepting the expression of accepting oneself as one is and not just with one's intellect, but of accepting oneself feelingly at the time: "This is me!" This is unaccompanied by fringe intellectualizations or judgments... that the feeling of liberation which occurs quite often after such strong experiences has something to do with a feeling of peace, a feeling of self-acceptance on a very deep emotional level, of being at one with oneself. It is really an experience of what we call the "real self." (Horney 1987, 99)

According to Zen philosophy, the true self is at One with the universe. There is no gap, no separation between ourselves and others. Be true to yourself and you return to the basis for ethical and compassionate action, the limitless source, not a narrow concept of self-image. Incorrect self-concepts and -images can lead to many of the discomforts with which we struggle. Interpersonal conflict is a reflection of the loss of harmony with the true self. Meditation helps us return to harmony.

The mental attitude of wholeheartedness can also be used as a source of therapeutic technique for therapists to help their patients. Dr. Horney advised therapists to put forth attention that is wholehearted, completely focused on the client. She explained:

> But what is self-evident is that the power of concentration is terribly important and can be trained. To illustrate, I want to read you a little example from one book on Zen Buddhism…Wholeheartedness of concentration means that all our faculties come into play: conscious reasoning, intuition, feelings, perception, curiosity, liking, sympathy, wanting to help, or whatever. (Horney 1987, 19)

Wholeheartedness can be directed to many activities of life, including interpersonal relationships at home and at work. But the first step comes from within, in wholeheartedness toward yourself. In fully accepting yourself here and now, you discover your true self. Then you can experience what Lin-chi meant when he said, "Nothing is missing."

Exercise in Wholehearted Attention

Sit comfortably with your eyes closed. Spend several moments bringing your attention into the present moment. Pay careful attention to what you are feeling. Try to listen fully to yourself, to encounter yourself deeply without any preconceptions. Can you notice what you are experiencing without judgment—without deciding that what you feel is good or bad, intelligent or ignorant? Simply listen and be fully present in the moment. What do you notice? Can you accept what is, whatever you feel, whether it is happy, sad, calm, tense, and so on and stay with it?

THE UNCONSCIOUS AND ZEN

Milton Erickson, M. D., a brilliant pioneer in the creative use of hypnosis in psychotherapy, believed that trust in the unconscious processes of both the patient and the therapist should be encouraged and cultivated. This became the basis for intervention to engage and enhance therapy, whether the difficulty was in character, attitude, life problem, or symptom. Erickson carefully trained and developed his students' unconscious abilities to enhance their skills. This meant that psychotherapy training sessions with Erickson were not just on the conscious level. He believed the unconscious level was more real and significant.

The unconscious is not something to be made conscious and controlled but rather to be embraced and engaged in, attentively. Awareness and control happen naturally when allowed. What does this mean? How, we might ask, can we act with awareness yet embrace the unconscious? Is this not a contradiction?

The unconscious is part of our everyday lives, and we do not think about it much unless it becomes a problem, or unless it is our business to think about it. Much of what we do, we do unconsciously, intuitively. Erickson liked to work intuitively. He had a deep respect for the mystery and wonder of life. He used to say that the actual reason for the patient's problem was a mystery, and often the solution was a mystery as well. No one can say just why the problem began or where it goes when it leaves. But explaining the difficulty is not what matters for therapy. The important concern is that patients over-come their problems and get on with living normal, and fulfilling lives. A great deal of time and money can be wasted searching for why. Change was more important to Erickson; explanations can come later. This point of view was central to Erickson's ability to help with a broad range of problems. He became renowned for his creativity and skill with impossible cases that traditional techniques could not affect. He enjoyed the opportunity to discover creative new ways to help.

Freud believed that the unconscious is where all deeper problems come from. He believed that the unconscious is a turbulent cauldron of instincts, impulses, and wishes: primitive and infantile. Conscious, rational functioning should predominate, according to Freud, in order to be civilized and sane. Thus, his cure for patients was for them to become more conscious, more aware of unconscious memories, wishes, and impulses. Then patients were encouraged to resolve their emotions, either by transforming their expression in positive ways or by learning to find mature satisfactions in reality. Many people today think of the unconscious in Freudian terms.

Erickson's concept of the unconscious is different from Freud's but similar to the Zen unconscious. Erickson thought of the unconscious as nonconscious, ever-present, deep within. He believed that the unconscious is healthy and natural, the source of our potential. As we go through life, we learn from the consequences of our efforts what we can and cannot do, what we are like and what our limits and capacities are. We develop conscious thoughts and beliefs. Some of them are accurate and useful, some are inaccurate and limiting. These conscious thoughts, beliefs, and concepts are where problems come from, not from the unconscious. Erickson believed that we should return to the unconscious, to the source of all that we are and can be. From the unconscious, as foundation, new abilities can emerge.

This accepting trust in the unconscious is parallel to Zen's view of the true nature, Mind with a capital M. Bodhidharma, Hui-neng, Lin-chi, Dogen, Hakuin—many of the great Zen masters shared this absolute faith in the deeper, inner nature. Hui-neng's disciple Shen-hui stated it clearly:

What is the Unconscious? It is not to think of being and nonbeing; it is not to think of good and bad; it is not to think of having limits or not having limits; it is not to think of measurements [or of nonmeasurements]; it is not to think of enlightenment, nor is it to think of being enlightened; it is not to think of Nirvana, nor is it to think of attaining Nirvana: this is the Unconscious. (D. T. Suzuki 1972, 61)

UNCONSCIOUS RESPONSE

Your unconscious intuitively knows things that you cannot recognize consciously. This exercise will help you experience unconscious knowing. Find a quiet place in your home or some other quiet area, where you will not be disturbed. Sit comfortably in a chair. Let your hands rest on your knees. Close your eyes and relax. Clear your mind of thought. Then focus your attention on your hands. Notice what you feel in your hands. Does one hand feel lighter or heavier than the other? Is one warmer or cooler? Notice what happens in your hands. Does one hand become even lighter, heavier, warmer, or cooler? You do not know what your unconscious will do. This is your unconscious response. Wait for the response and enjoy the discovery. Now open your eyes and return to your usual conscious functioning.

Unconscious Meditation

Sit comfortably, quietly, and allow your thoughts to drift. Do not think about anything in particular. Simply allow your breathing to relax, and your muscles to be comfortable as you sit in meditation. Do not pay attention to anything in particular. Let your unconscious be your guide, beyond thought, judgment, simply being and accepting what your unconscious presents. Stay with this until you feel ready to stop.

EMPTINESS: FACING THE VOID

After a period of time in deep therapy, many people often come to a crisis point, an impasse. They have set aside their assumptions about the world and instead have wholeheartedly accepted here-and-now experiencing. Then, all the old ways of behaving and thinking somehow do not feel right anymore; they do not work. These people cannot quite stay as they are, and they cannot quite go back to what was. Yet what lies ahead is unknown, uncharted territory. They describe the experience as entering a void, an emptiness. One client said it was like being adrift in the middle of the ocean, not moving forward and not moving backward. What helps them carry through is not just concepts, other people's opinions, past experience, or future hopes. What must be faced is moment-to-moment awareness and acceptance of the emptiness.

Meditation on the Void

Meditate on what you experience. Start where you are. Follow the flow of your awareness, without judgment, accepting what you feel. Contemplate the phrase "form is emptiness and emptiness is form." Now think of an empty void in the Zen sense: a void that is not nothing but rather is no-thing—changing process, coming to be, a fertile void of possibility. By staying with the emptiness of life's changing conditions, you may discover new form—and in the process a healthier, more awake and alive you.

The wellspring of positive potential is unconscious within each of us, beyond any ideas we might have about ourselves. When we calm ourselves and return to this, we regain our spontaneous, creative, flexible true nature. Life gains new meaning.

CONCLUSIONS

The form of Zen was always changed by the culture that embraced it. In turn, Zen changed the form of the culture. The Chinese interpreted Indian Buddhism through their Taoist/Confucianist background and, ultimately, created Zen. The Japanese found Zen useful, as they transformed it into a practical expression of their artistic spirit. Now, we in the West can harmonize Zen with our individuality, part of the Oneness.

The waters of Zen are as limitless as they are formless. Form is emptiness, emptiness is form. Emptiness has great potential, discovered through meditation. Meditation enriches your inner spirit, grounding you firmly in the enlightened perspective to guide you in how to reach your potential.

Through meditation, the sum and substance of Zen, you learn how to attune to your intuitive nature, to live at one with yourself and your life. Zen arts offer a way to do Zen through active involvement in a skill or in creating. You become meditatively aware by immersion in all your actions. Then this way of approaching your art becomes your way of living an enlightened life.

Engage yourself fully in your life and your talents can develop to their full potential. You create your everyday life anew with everything you feel and do. You get more out of what you do by simply living Zen, moment by moment!

Although the unmapped way may twist and wind,
Your steps will find sure footing
In the vast unknown, with the potential of Mind.
—C. Alexander Simpkins

CHINA
Early T'ang Dynasty

Bodhidharma
First Patriarch of Zen
d. 532

•

Hui-k'o (Jap. Eka)
Second Patriarch
487 – 593

•

Seng ts'an (Jap. Sosan)
Third Patriarch
d. 606

•

Tao-hsin (Jap. Doshin)
Fourth Patriarch
580 – 651

•

Hung-jen (Jap. Guinin)
Fifth Patriarch
601 – 674

HUNG-JEN

Shen-hsiu (Jap. Jinshu)
Sixth Patriarch (Northern School)
605 – 706

•

P'u chi (Jap. Fujaku)
(Northern School)
651 – 739

•

Tao-hsuan (Jap. Dosen)
702 – 760

Hui-neng (Jap. Eno)
Sixth Patriarch (Southern School)
638 – 713

•

Nan-Yueh Huai-jang
(Jap. Nangaku Ejo)
677 – 744

•

Ma-tsu Tao-i (Jap. Baso Doitsu)
709 – 788

•

Pai-chang Huai-hai
(Jap. Hyakujo Ekai)
720 – 814

•

Huang-po Hsi-yun
(Jap. Obaku Kiun)
d. 850

•

Lin-chi I-hsuan★
(Jap. Rinzai Gigen)
d. 866

LATER T'ANG DYNASTY
THE FIVE HOUSES

A.& B. House of Yun-men and Fa-yen
Ummon & Hogen
Hsueh-feng I-ts'un
Seppo Gison
822 – 908

Two generations	Yun-men Wen-yen
•	(Jap. Ummon Bun'en)
Fa yen Wen-i (Jap. Hogen Bun'eki)	864 – 949
885 – 958	

C. HOUSE OF KUEI-YANG
IGYO
Kuei-shan Ling-yu (Jap. Issan Reiyu)
771 – 853

D. HOUSE OF LIN-CHI
Rinzai
Lin-chi I'hsuan (Jap. Rinzai Gigen)
d. 866

•

Six generations

Yang-ch'i Fang-hui
(Jap. Yogi Hoe)
921 – 1049

Huang-lung Hui-nan
(Jap. Oryo Enan)
1002 – 1069

E. HOUSE OF TS'AO-TUNG
SOTO
Tung-shan Liang-chieh (Jap. Tozan Ryokai)
807 – 869

Many generations

•

Tan-hsia Tzu-ch'un
(Jap. Tanka Shijun)
d. 1119

Ts'ao-shan Pen-chi
(Jap. Sozan Honjaku)
840 – 901

(Soto school formed from combined efforts of
Tozan and Sozan.)

SUNG DYNASTY
Rinzai School

Yang-ch'i Fang-hui

Six generations	Two generations
•	•
Wu-men Hui-k'ai	Yuan-wu K'och'in
(Jap. Mumon Ekai)	(Jap. Engo Kukugon)
1183 – 1260	1063 – 1135
Compiler of the Wu-men-Kuan	Compiler of *Hekiganroku*
(Jap. Mumonkan)	•
•	Ta-hui Tsung-kao
Shinchi Kakushin	(Jap. Daie Soko)
1207 – 1298	1089 – 1163

HUNG-LUNG HUI-NAN
•

Two generations
•

Eisai
1141 – 1215
Transmitted the Rinzai School to Japan

TAN-HSIA TZU-CH'UN

Three generations

•

T'ien-t'ung Ji-ching (Jap. Tendo Nyojo)
1163 – 1228

•

Dogen Kigen
1200 – 1253
(Transmitted Soto Zen to Japan)

JAPAN
Main Line of Rinzai School

Nampo Joymo
1235 – 1309
First to nationalize Ch'an from China into Japanese Zen
•
Shuho Myocho
1282 – 1338

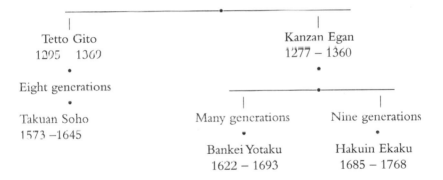

Tetto Gito
1295   1369
•
Eight generations
•
Takuan Soho
1573 –1645

Kanzan Egan
1277 – 1360
•

Many generations
•
Bankei Yotaku
1622 – 1693

Nine generations
•
Hakuin Ekaku
1685 – 1768

Main Line of Soto

Dogen Kigen
1200 – 1253

•

Koun Ejo
1198 – 1280

•

Tettsu Gikai
1219 – 1309

•

Keizan Jokin
1268 – 1325

•

Gasan Joseki
1275 – 1365

•

This line continues to modern times.

Modern Period
Japan to America

Hakuin Ekaku
1685 – 1768

•

Gasan Jitto
1727 – 1797

•

Inan Ien
1751 — 1814

•

Taigen Shigen
1768 — 1837

•

Gisan Zenrai
1822 — 1899

•

Kosen Soon
1816 — 1892

•

Kogaku Soen (Shaku Soyen)
1859 — 1919
First to introduce Zen to the West in 1893

Tettuso Sokatsu
1870 — 1954

•

Sasaki Shigetsu
1882 — 1945
Founded first Zen institute
in New York
Married to American
Ruth Fuller Sasaki

D. T. Suzuki
1870 — 1966
Translator/student

•

Senzaki Nyogen
1876 — 1958
First Zen master to
come to U.S.

KOREA

Won Hyo (617 – 618) popularizer of Buddhism in Korea

•

Ma-tsu (China)

•

One generation

•

Toui (d. 825) first to bring Zen to Korea. Founder of Purim-
SaTemple, first of the Nine Mountain Schools of Korea

•

Chinul (1150 – 1210) developed Suden Enlightenment-Gradual Cultivation
theory for unification of schools as Chogye Order

•

T'aego Pou (1301 – 1382) encouraged unification further under
King Kongmin's decree (1325)

•

Seung Sahn (b. 1927) taught Korean Zen widely in America,
Europe, and Canada

BIBLIOGRAPHY

Abe, M., ed. 1986. *A Zen Life. D. T. Suzuki Remembered*. New York. Weatherhill.

Abe, M. 1992. *A Study of Dogen*. Albany: State University of New York Press.

Awakawa, Y. 1981. *Zen Painting*. New York: Kodansha International.

Benoit, H. 1990. *Zen and the Psychology of Transformation*. Rochester, Vt.: Inner Traditions International.

Blofeld, J. 1994. *The Chinese Art of Tea*. London: George Allen & Unwin.

Blyth, R.H. 1964. *Zen and Zen Classics*, vols. 1 and 2. Tokyo: Hokuseido Press.

———. 1966. *Haiku: Summer-Autumn*, vol. 2. Tokyo: Hokuseido.

———. 1968. *Haiku: Spring*, vol. 3. Tokyo: Hokuseido.

———. 1968. *Haiku: Autumn & Winter*, vol. 4. Tokyo: Hokuseido.

———. 1969. *Haiku: Eastern Culture*, vol. 1. Tokyo: Hokuseido.

Buswell, R. 1991. *Tracing Back the Radiance*. Honolulu, Hawaii: University of Hawaii Press.

Cage, J. 1961. *Silence*. Middletown, Conn.: Wesleyan University Press.

———. 1967. *A Year from Monday*. Middletown, Conn.: Wesleyan University Press.

Conze, E., I. Horner, D. Snellgrove, and A. Waley, eds. 1995. *Buddhist Texts Through the Ages*. Oxford, Engl.: Oneworld Publications.

Dumoulin, H. 1988. *Zen Buddhism: A History*, vol. 1. New York: Macmillan Publishing Co.

———. 1990. *Zen Buddhism: A History*, vol. 2. New York: Macmillan Publishing Co.

Erickson, M. July 10-15, 1979. Personal meeting. Phoenix, Arizona.

Frank, J. D. 1991. *Persuasion and Healing*. Baltimore: The Johns Hopkins University Press.

Graham, A. 1968. *Conversations: Christian and Buddhist: Encounters in Japan*. New York: Harcourt Brace & World, Inc.

———. 1974. *Contemplative Christianity*. New York: Harcourt Brace & World.

Hall, E. 1983. *The Dance of Life*. New York: Anchor Press/Doubleday.

Hamilton, E. 1961. *The Collected Dialogues of Plato*. Princeton, N.J.: Princeton University Press.

Henderson, H. 1977. *Haiku in English*. Rutland, Vt.: Charles E. Tuttle Co., Inc.

Herregel, G. 1958. *Zen in the Art of Flower Arrangement*. London: Arkana.

Herrigel, E. 1971a. *The Method of Zen*. New York: Vintage Books.

———. 1971b. *Zen in the Art of Archery*. New York: Vintage Books.

Higginson, W. 1996. *The Haiku Seasons*. Toyko: Kodansha International.

Hirai, T. 1974. *Psychophysiology of Zen*. Tokyo: Igaku Shoin.

Horney, K. 1964. *The Neurotic Personality of Our Time*. New York: W.W. Norton & Co.

———. 1987. *Final Lectures*. New York: W.W. Norton & Co.

Ifrah, G. 1987. *From One to Zero, A Universal History of Numbers*. New York: Penguin Books.

Keel, Hee-Sung. 1984. *Chinul: The Founder of Korean Son Tradition*. Berkeley, Calif.: Berkeley Buddhist Studies Series.

Kitagawa, J. 1966. *Religion in Japanese History*. New York: Columbia University Press.

Kubie, L. 1975. *Neurotic Distortion of the Creative Process.* Toronto: The Noonday Press.

Lee, Bruce. 1979. *Tao of Jeet Kune Do.* Burbank, Calif.: Ohara Publications.

Leggett, T. 1958. *The Warrior Koans. Early Zen in Japan.* London: Arkana.

Mattson, G. E. 1963. *The Way of Karate.* Rutland, Vt.: Charles E. Tuttle Co., Inc.

Musashi, M. 1974. *The Book of Five Rings.* Woodstock, N.Y.: The Overlook Press.

Nitobe, I. 1969. *Bushido: The Soul of Japan.* Boston: Charles E. Tuttle, Co., Inc.

Okakura, Kakuzo. 1989. *The Book of Tea.* New York: Kodansha.

Parulski, G. 1976. *A Path to Oriental Wisdom.* Burbank, Calif.: Ohara Publications, Inc.

Perls, F. 1969. *Gestalt Therapy Verbatim.* Lafayette, Calif.: Real People Press.

———. 1969b. *In and Out the Garbage Pail.* Lafayette, Calif.: Real People Press.

Pine, R. 1989. *The Zen Teaching of Bodhidharma.* San Francisco: North Point Press.

Price, A. F., and W. Mou-lam. 1990. *The Diamond Sutra and the Sutra of Hui-Neng.* Boston: Shambala.

Reps, P. 1994. *Zen Flesh, Zen Bones.* Rutland, Vt.: Charles E. Tuttle Co., Inc.

Ross, N. W. 1960. *The World of Zen.* New York: Vintage.

Sadler, A. L. 1994. *Cha-No-Yu. The Japanese Tea Ceremony.* Rutland, Vt.: Charles E. Tuttle Co., Inc.

Sasaki, R. F. 1965. *The Zen Koan.* San Diego: Harcourt Brace Jovanovich Publishers.

———. 1975. *The Recorded Sayings of Chían Master Lin-chi Hui-chao of Chen Prefecture.* Kyoto, Japan: The Institute of Zen Studies.

———. 1992. *The Whole World is a Single Flower.* Boston: Charles E. Tuttle Co., Inc.

Sekida, K. 1977. *Two Zen Classics: Mumonkan & Hekiganroku.* New York: Weatherhill.

Seung Sahn. 1992. *Only Don't Know.* Cumberland, R.I.: Primary Point Press.

Shigematsu, S. 1988. *A Zen Harvest.* San Francisco: North Point Press. Shibayama, 1993.

Simpkins, C. A., and A. M. Simpkins. 1996. *Principles of Meditation: Eastern Wisdom for the Western Mind.* Boston: Charles E. Tuttle Co., Inc.

———. 1992. *The Whole World is a Single Flower.* Boston: Charles E. Tuttle Co., Inc.

———. 1997. *Living Meditation: From Principle to Practice.* Boston: Charles E. Tuttle Co., Inc.

———. 1998. *Meditation From Thought to Action.* Boston: Charles E. Tuttle Co., Inc.

———. 1997b. *Zen Around the World: A 2500 Year Journey from the Buddha to You.* Boston: Charles E. Tuttle Co., Inc.

———. 1990. *Principles of Self Hypnosis: Pathways to the Unconscious.* New York: Irvington.

Skinner, B. F. *Cognition, Creativity, and Behavior.* Film.

Soyen, Shaku. 1987. *Zen for Americans.* New York: Dorset Press.

Stevens, J. *The Sword of No-Sword.* Boston: Shambala, 1989.

Stevens, J. O., ed. 1975. *Gestalt Is.* Moab, Utah: Real People Press.

Suzuki, D.T. 1955. *Studies in Zen.* New York: Philosophical Library.

———. 1960. *Manual of Zen Buddhism.* New York: Grove Weidenfeld.

———. 1994. *The Training of the Zen Buddhist Monk.* Boston: Charles E. Tuttle Co., Inc.

———. 1972. *The Zen Doctrine of No-Mind.* York Beach: Samuel Weiser, Inc.

———. 1973. *Zen and Japanese Culture.* Princeton, N.J.: Princeton University Press.

———. 1994. *The Zen Koan as a Means of Attaining Enlightenment.* Boston: Charles E. Tuttle Co., Inc.

Suzuki, S. 1979. *Zen Mind, Beginners Mind*. New York: Weatherhill.

Takuan, S. 1986. *The Unfettered Mind*. Tokyo: Kodansha International.

Thompson, K. 1968. *Japanese Ink-painting as Taught by Ukai Uchiyama*. Rutland, Vt.: Charles E. Tuttle Co., Inc.

Waddell, N. 1994a. *The Essential Teachings of Zen Master Hakuin*. Boston: Shambala.

———. 1994b. *The Unborn: The Life and Teaching of Zen Master Bankei 1622–1693*. San Francisco: North Point Press.

Watson, Burton. 1993. *The Zen Teachings of Master Lin-Chi*. Boston: Shambala.

Watterson, Bill. 1990. *Weirdos From Another Planet*. New York: Andrews and McMeel.

Watts, A. 1960. *This Is It*. New York: Vintage.

———. 1961. *Psychotherapy East and West*. New York: Ballantine Books.

Westgeest, Z. 1996. *Zen in the Fifties*. Amstelveen: Waanders Uitgevers, Zwolle, Cobra museum voor moderne Kunst.

Yamada, S. 1966. *Complete Sumi-e Techniques*. Elmsford, NY: Japan Publications Trading Company.

Yamamoto, Tsunetomo. 1979. *The Book of the Samurai Hagakure*. Tokyo: Kodansha International Ltd.

Yampolsky, Philip. 1971. *The Zen Master Hakuin: Selected Writings*. New York: Columbia University Press.

Yokoi, Huko. 1990. *Zen Master Dogen*. New York: Weatherhill.

Simple Zen Art

Buddha, on page 2
Chinese, Northern Wei dynasty
Limestone, first quarter, Sixth century
San Diego Museum of Art (Gift of the Asian Arts Committee)

Landscape depicting setting for Zen monasteries deep in the woods, on page 8
Chi Chi-Chia, Chinese, Seventeenth century
Ink and color on silk, 1677
San Diego Museum of Art

Fukurokuju, on page 24
Hakuin, Japanese (1685 – 1768)
Ink on paper
San Diego Museum of Art (Museum purchase
through the Charlotte Webster Memorial Fund)

Zen Circle, on page 54
Tomikichiro Tokurik
Woodblock print

Treasure Peak, on page 84
Sokuhi, Obaku (1616 – 1671)
Japanese (b. China)
Ink on hanging scroll
San Diego Museum of Art (Museum Purchase)

Jittoku, on page 108
Toban Unkoku, Japanese, Mid-seventeenth century
Ink on paper
San Diego Museum of Art (Bequest of Earle W. Grant)

Ox, on page 110
Tomikichiro Tokurik
Woodblock print

Ho–tei, the happy monk, on page 120
Seventeenth Century
Ink on hanging scroll
(Private collection, Simpkins)

Simpkins, C. Alexander.
    Simple Zen : a guide to living moment by moment / C. Alexander
Simpkins & Annellen M. Simpkins.
        p. cm.
    Includes bibliographical references.
    ISBN 0-8048-3174-2 (pb)
    1. Spiritual life--Zen Buddhism. I. Simpkins, Annellen M.
II. Title
BQ9288.S57 1999
294.3'927--dc21   99-24270
                                             CIP